Cover-up

Government Spin or Truth?

All Scripture quotations are from the King James Version of the Holy Bible.

Printed in the United States of America

ISBN 1-57558-125-6

Cover-up

Government Spin or Truth?

Connecting the dots—
September 11 . . . Iraq . . .
and Our Vanishing
Constitutional Rights

Dennis Laurence Cuddy, Ph.D.

Dedicated to
the memory of
those whose lives were cut short
by the tragic attacks of
September 11, 2001,
and to
their loved ones left behind
and all who sincerely
love our Republic
and cherish its Constitution

The following excerpts are from Gore Vidal's "The Enemy Within" published in the (London) *Observer*, October 27, 2002:

In December 1998, CIA director George Tenet wrote to his deputies that "we are at war" with Osama bin Laden. So impressed was the FBI by his warnings that by 20 September 2001, "the FBI still had only one analyst assigned full time to al-Qaeda." . . . December 20, 2000, Clinton's outgoing team devised a plan to strike al-Qaeda in retaliation for the assault on the warship *Cole*. Clinton's National Security Advisor, Sandy Berger, personally briefed his successor on the plan but [Condoleezza] Rice, still very much in her role as director of Chevron-Texaco, with special duties regarding Pakistan and Uzbekistan, now denies any such briefing. A year and a half later (12 August 2002) fearless *Time* magazine reported this odd memory lapse. . . . In order to bring this evildoer [bin Laden] to justice ("dead or alive"), Afghanistan, the object of the exercise, was made safe not only for democracy but for Union Oil of California whose proposed pipeline from Turkmenistan to Afghanistan to Pakistan and the Indian Ocean port of Karachi, had been abandoned under the Taliban's chaotic regime. Currently, the pipeline is a go-project thanks to the [Cheney-Bush] junta's installation of Unocal employee [John J. Maresca] as U.S. envoy to the newly born democracy whose president, Hamid Karzai, is also, according to *Le Monde*, a former employee of a Unocal subsidiary. Conspiracy? Coincidence! Once Afghanistan looked to be within the fold, the junta, which had managed to pull off a complex diplomatic-military caper, abruptly replaced Osama, the personification of evil, with Saddam. This has been hard to explain since there is nothing to connect Iraq with 9/11 . . . [and] there are stories in the press about the vast wealth of Iraq which must—for the sake of the free world—be reassigned to U.S. and European consortiums. . . . Post 9/11, the American media were filled with preemptory denunciations of unpatriotic "conspiracy theorists," who not only are always with us but are usually easy for the media to discredit since it is an article of faith that there are no conspiracies in American life. Yet, a year or so ago, who would have thought that most of corporate America had been conspiring with accountants to cook their books. . . . Apparently, "conspiracy stuff" is now shorthand for unspeakable truth. . . . By law, the fighters [fighter planes] should have been up at around 8:15 [on September 11, 2001]. If they had, all the hijacked planes might have been diverted or shot down. . . . Certainly, the one-hour 20-minute failure to put fighter planes in the air could not have been due to a breakdown throughout the entire Air Force along the East Coast. Mandatory standard operational procedure had been told to cease and desist. . . ."

Introduction

Since my *September 11 Prior Knowledge* book was published, a great deal of additional information has come to light concerning the subject. There have been, and will be, investigations, and basic questions that need to be answered by our government. For example, why on September 10, 2001, would some top Pentagon officials suddenly cancel their travel plans for the next morning because of security concerns unless they had specific, credible information an attack was about to occur?

> The state of alert had been high during the past two weeks, and a particularly urgent warning may have been received the night before the attacks, causing some Pentagon brass to cancel a trip. Why that same information was not available to the 266 people who died aboard the four hijacked commercial aircraft may become a hot topic on the [Capitol] Hill.
>
> —*Newsweek*, September 13, 2001

> On September 10, *Newsweek* has learned, a group of top Pentagon officials suddenly canceled travel plans for the next morning, apparently because of security concerns.
>
> —*Newsweek*, September 24, 2001

If government officials had information that an attack was about to occur, why wasn't the public warned? Has our government been telling us the whole truth, or have some in our government been giving us "spin," covering up certain important information? This sequel to *September 11 Prior Knowledge* looks at questions like these and other contemporaneous issues, such as a possible war with Iraq and our vanishing constitutional rights, supposedly necessary to protect us from terrorism.

Part I

New information is constantly being revealed concerning the September 11, 2001, attacks upon America, and especially insightful is relevant information that could be classified under "what the government hasn't told us." For example, the government didn't tell us that the downing of TWA Flight 800 on July 17, 1996, was a terrorist attack, according to Yossef Bodansky, author of *Bin Laden* (1999) and director of the U.S. House of Representatives Task Force on Terrorism and Unconventional Warfare. Bodansky said that

> the case of TWA 800 served as a turning point because of Washington's determination and to a great extent ability to suppress terrorist explanations and "float" mechanical failure theories. To avoid such suppression after future strikes, terrorism-sponsoring states would raise the ante so that the West cannot ignore them.

On September 11, 2001, the "ante" was raised with the attacks upon the World Trade Center and the Pentagon. And on February 4, 2003, *First Strike: TWA 800 and the Attack on America* by Jack Cashill and James Sanders was published as a Thomas Nelson imprint by WND (*WorldNetDaily*) Books. On this same day, *WorldNetDaily* published "TWA 800 cover-up led to 9–11 attacks?" about the book, stating that

> Cashill and Sanders have uncovered startling new evidence about the crash, including a critical Islamic terrorist connection covered

up by federal investigators to give America a false sense of peace leading to the presidential elections three months later [in November 1996]. Ordinary Americans never realized it, but on July 17, 1996, the U.S. was on the highest state of alert since the Cuban missile crisis, *First Strike* shows. . . . The Islamic Change Movement [took] responsibility for the attack [on TWA 800], [and] predicted such an attack in advance. This is the same group that had taken responsibility for Khobar Towers, now widely blamed on al-Qaeda. "The mujahedin will deliver the ultimate response to the threats of the foolish American president," the communique predicted earlier July 17. "Everyone will be amazed at the size of that response. . . . Their time is at the morning-dawn. Is not the morning-dawn near?" Dawn in Afghanistan, the authors point out, corresponded almost exactly to dusk in New York. The next day, the Islamic Change Movement issued another communique: "We carried out our promise with the plane attack of yesterday," it said in part.

Concerning the mastermind of the September 11, 2001, attacks, Osama bin Laden helped the Kosovo Liberation Army (KLA), formerly classified by the U.S. State Department as a terrorist organization. What haven't we been told about the KLA and Yugoslavia? In his article "We Created a Monster" (Toronto *Globe and Mail*, July 31, 2001), former Canadian ambassador to Yugoslavia James Bissett revealed:

When Canadian pilots joined in the NATO bombing of Yugoslavia in March of 1999, we were told . . . that the NATO intervention in Kosovo was necessary to prevent the violence there from spreading and destabilizing the Balkans. Yet we now know that, long before the bombing, NATO countries were inciting violence in Kosovo and attempting to destabilize that Serbian province. . . . Media reports have revealed that as early as 1998, the Central Intelligence Agency, assisted by the British Special Armed Services, were arming and training Kosovo Liberation Army members in Albania to foment armed rebellion in Kosovo. The KLA terrorists were sent back into Kosovo to assassinate Serbian mayors, ambush Serbian policemen, and do everything possible to incite murder and chaos. . . . After bombing Yugoslavia into submission, NATO then stood by and submissively allowed the KLA to murder, pillage, and burn. . . .

Do you think the U.S. will press for leaders of the KLA to be brought before an international war crimes tribunal? Don't count on it. Similarly, on Sunday, August 18, 2002, *Newsweek* reported that a confidential U.N. memorandum found evidence that would justify a "full-fledged criminal investigation" into the suffocation deaths of hundreds of Taliban prisoners held by the U.S.-backed Northern Alliance in Afghanistan. In the Associated Press story about this on Fox News (August 18, 2002), one learns that

> in Boston, the group Physicians for Human Rights, which also sent a team to investigate the reported massacre, said it had repeatedly asked the governments of the United States and Afghanistan as well as the United Nations to secure the gravesite and launch a comprehensive criminal investigation. "The refusal of the United States to acknowledge and investigate the possibility that its military partner murdered hundreds or thousands of prisoners is a terrible repudiation of its commitment to hold perpetrators of war crimes accountable for their deeds," Leonard S. Rubenstein, executive director of Physicians for Human Rights, said in a statement released Sunday.

Pertaining to the creation of another "monster," the Taliban, *Christian Science Monitor* writer John Cooley in *Unholy Wars: Afghanistan, America, and International Terrorism* (1999) revealed that "two Islamic powers, Saudi Arabia and Pakistan, allied with the 'world's only remaining superpower,' the United States, by 1994 to hatch a monster of Islamist extremism, the Taliban movement." (Cooley also described the working relationship between the CIA and Pakistan's intelligence service [ISI], the CIA and drug smuggling, and the CIA and the notorious Bank for Credit and Commerce International [BCCI].) Similarly, over six months prior to September 11, 2001, the *Times of India* on March 7, 2001, published "CIA worked in tandem with Pak to create Taliban," which begins with the following statement: "The Central Intelligence Agency (CIA) worked in tandem with Pakistan to create the 'monster' that is today Afghanistan's ruling Taliban, a leading U.S. expert on South Asia said here." The expert, Selig Harrison from the Woodrow Wilson International Centre for Scholars, also said "the CIA still has close links with the ISI (Pakistan's Inter-Services Intelligence)." Related to this, in "U.S. Saudi Scandal" (*NOW Toronto*, November 22–28, 2001) by Alex Roslin, one finds that Wayne Madsen, formerly with the U.S. National Security Agency, explained: "You had an American pro-Taliban faction [inside the U.S. government]. They were totally in bed with the Taliban." And further along these lines, Congressman Dana Rohrbacher, during hearings before the House Committee on International Relations on July 12, 2000, remarked:

> . . . I have stated that I believe there is a covert policy by this [Clinton] Administration, a shameful covert policy of supporting the Taliban. . . . Although the Administration has denied supporting the Taliban, it is clear that they discouraged all of the anti-Taliban supporters from supporting the efforts in Afghanistan to defeat the Taliban. . . . This Administration has acted in a way that has kept the Taliban in power. . . . At a time when the Taliban were vulnerable, the top person in this Administration, Mr. [Karl] Inderfurth and Bill Richardson personally went to Afghanistan and convinced . . . all of the anti-Taliban forces and their supporters to disarm and to cease their flow of support for the anti-Taliban forces. . . .

However, after these hearings in the summer and fall of 2000, a shift in policy occurred. The Taliban had gotten rid of most of the poppy/opium production and was looking for American financial help for having done so. But on October 12, the *U.S.S. Cole* was attacked, and the U.S. became less interested in poppies than in getting Osama bin Laden. The Taliban feared what might happen to them if they tried to apprehend bin Laden and turn him over to the U.S. So, at that point, without the large amount of financial assistance from the U.S. for which the Taliban hoped, bin Laden himself became an important source of income for the Taliban. S. Frederick Starr (chairman of the Central Asia-Caucasus Institute at Johns Hopkins' Nitze School of Advanced International Studies) writing "Afghanistan Land Mine" in the *Washington Post* (December 19, 2000) revealed that

> the United States has quietly begun to align itself with those in the Russian government calling for military action against Afghanistan and has toyed with the idea of a new raid to wipe out Osama bin Laden. Until it backed off under local pressure, it went so far as to explore whether a Central Asian country would permit the use of its territory for such a purpose. . . . Assistant Secretary of State Karl Inderfurth met recently with Russia's friends in the government of India to discuss what kind of government should replace the Taliban. Thus, while claiming to oppose a military solution to the Afghan problem, the United States is now talking about the overthrow of a regime that controls nearly the entire country, in the hope it can be replaced with a hypothetical government that does not exist even on paper. . . . The United States is supporting a one-sided resolution in the United Nations that would strengthen sanctions against foreign military aid for the Taliban but take no action against its warlord opponents.

About seven months later, Karl "Rick" Inderfurth was one of a three-member delegation that met in July 2001 in Berlin and warned the Taliban that the U.S. might consider military action against them if they did not comply with American government wishes. Also concerning Inderfurth, Bill Gertz in *Breakdown* (2002) wrote:

Inderfurth was a special assistant to Madeleine Albright, who was the U.S. ambassador to the United Nations during President [Bill] Clinton's second term. Inderfurth was a proponent of Albright's policy of "assertive multilateralism," the liberal notion that the United States should not be the leader of the free world but should let the United Nations take the lead. Inderfurth was also a major proponent of sharing classified U.S. intelligence information with the United Nations.

While the Clinton administration earlier was conducting activities which amounted to support for the Taliban (and Pakistan, which helped create the Taliban's authority in Afghanistan), in 1996 the president of the Sudan offered to arrest Osama bin Laden and supply intelligence about other terrorist groups (which included two of the hijackers of September 11, 2001). According to Bill Gertz in *Breakdown*, though, "the offer of Sudanese assistance evaporated in August 1998 when President Clinton ordered U.S. military forces to destroy the pharmaceutical plant in Sudan that was suspected of being a chemical arms factory. The only problem was that later evidence showed that the plant was probably *not* an arms factory."

At this same time, according to Dana Priest and Dan Eggen in "9/11 Probers Say Agencies Failed to Heed Attack Signs" (*Washington Post*, September 19, 2002),

The FAA and FBI were told in August 1998 that a group of unidentified Arabs planned to fly an airplane loaded with explosives into the World Trade Center from a foreign country. . . . In December 1998, an intelligence assessment concluded that bin Laden "is actively planning against U.S. targets . . . keenly interested in striking the U.S. on its own soil." . . . In a Dec. 4, 1998, memo to his deputies, CIA director George J. Tenet issued guidance "declaring, in effect, war" with bin Laden.

On August 20, 1998, the U.S. fired at least twenty cruise missiles at three or more al-Qaeda training camps in Afghanistan in retaliation for al-Qaeda's bombings of American embassies in Kenya and Tanzania on August 7. And in Douglas Waller's "Inside the Hunt for Osama" (*Time*, December 21, 1998), one reads that "intelligence sources tell *Time* they have evidence that bin Laden may be planning his boldest move yet—a strike on Washington or possibly New York City in an eye-for-an-eye retaliation. 'We've hit his headquarters, now he hits ours,' says a State Department aide."

Also pertaining to August 1998, in Barton Gellman's article "Broad Effort Launched After '98 Attacks" (*Washington Post*, December 19, 2001), it was revealed that beginning on August 7, 1998, not only did President Clinton authorize covert action, but he also "signed three highly classified Memoranda of Notification expanding the available tools. In succession, the president authorized killing instead of capturing bin Laden, then added several of al-Qaeda's senior lieutenants, and finally approved the shooting down of private civilian aircraft on which they flew." Knowing this, it is difficult to understand why President George W. Bush announced after the September 11, 2001, attacks that we were going to war against the terrorists. It would seem that the U.S. and the terrorists had been at war with each other for a long time already. And if the president of another country had authorized the shooting down of private civilian aircraft on which Americans flew, wouldn't we consider that tantamount to a declaration of war against the U.S.? Thus, it should have been a surprise to no one that on June 23, 2001, the Reuters news agency distributed a report headlined "Bin Laden Fighters Plan Anti-U.S. Attack," which led with the following statement: "Followers of exiled Saudi dissident Osama bin Laden are planning a major attack on U.S. and Israeli interests."

Still, it should be remembered that early in the administration of President George W. Bush, there were negotiations with the Taliban, and the possibility of working with them was even considered after the September 11 attacks. According to Bill Gertz in *Breakdown*, shortly after the U.S. launched its military operation against the Taliban following these terrorist attacks, Abdul Haq (a folk hero among the Pashtun tribes in Afghanistan) advised American officials via Robert Mc-Farlane (national security advisor to President Reagan) that he could rally the Pashtuns in southern Afghanistan and oust the Taliban. But not only did U.S. army general Tommy Franks (commander in chief of the U.S. Central Command) refuse to help Haq, the CIA refused as well. As Gertz relates it, "The CIA rebuffed appeals from McFarlane and Haq. 'We received only dismissive comments and indifference,' McFarlane said. 'In one astonishing exchange we were told, to paraphrase, "We don't yet have our marching orders concerning U.S. policy; it may be that we will end up dealing with the Taliban."'" Perhaps relevant to this is James Bone's article, "U.S. 'let Taliban men escape,'" in *The* (London) *Times* (January 21, 2001), in which he revealed:

> The United States secretly approved rescue flights by Pakistan into Kunduz that let Taliban leaders and al-Qaeda fighters escape from the besieged northern Afghan city before its fall last year, *New Yorker* magazine reports today. . . . "What was supposed to be a limited evacuation apparently slipped out of control and, as an unintended consequence, an unknown number of Taliban and al-Qaeda fighters managed to join in the exodus," the magazine reports.

Regarding the "unintended" nature of these rescue flight results, it is difficult to believe that the U.S. government never considered the possibility that Taliban and al-Qaeda members might flee in this manner.

Relevant to the story above, J. S. Newton of the *Fayetteville Observer* wrote in "Officials Deny bin Laden Escaped November Capture" (August 2, 2002):

A Special Forces soldier says that troops had Osama bin Laden pinpointed in Afghanistan in November, but leaders took too long to decide to go after him and he slipped away. . . . The soldier [said] he was on the ground at Tora Bora when bin Laden was located. . . . The soldier said bin Laden's captured cook had told American military officials bin Laden's exact location. But a Special Forces team captain on the ground would not give approval to go after bin Laden because there was no specific mission order to do so, the soldier said. While the Army was deciding what to do, Special Forces soldiers saw two Russian-made helicopters fly into the area where bin Laden was believed to be, load up passengers, and fly toward Pakistan. "I said, 'There he goes,'" the soldier said.

Coincidentally, Fayetteville (Fort Bragg), North Carolina-based Joint Special Operations Command (Delta Force) has a fleet of aircraft, even former Soviet helicopters, the bulk of which now fly from airfields in Uzbekistan and two Pakistani air bases, Shahbaz and Shamsi.

The reason offered by the U.S. government for going to war with the Taliban was their refusal after September 11, 2001, to turn over Osama bin Laden and his al-Qaeda members. This is curious, though, given that in Thomas Walkom's "Did bin Laden have help from U.S. friends?" (*Toronto Star*, November 27, 2001), we learn that

the Taliban's unprecedented offer to extradite bin Laden to a third country, well before the Sept. 11 attacks, was reported in the *Times* of London in February. . . . Earlier this month, *The Guardian*, a U.K. newspaper, reported that FBI agents had been told by the Bush administration to back off investigating members of the bin Laden clan in the U.S. In September, the *Wall Street Journal* documented the lucrative business connections between the bin Laden family and senior U.S. Republicans, including the president's father, George Bush, Sr. What are we to make of all of this? One possible conclusion is that the bin Laden terror problem was allowed to get out of hand because bin Laden, himself, had powerful protectors in both Washington and Saudi Arabia. If that's true, no wonder the Bush administration prefers that he be killed rather than allowed to testify in open court.

Then, concerning the period immediately after the September 11 attacks, John Pilger in "This war of lies goes on" (English *Daily Mirror*, November 16, 2001) related that

in late September and early October, leaders of Pakistan's two Islamic parties negotiated bin Laden's extradition to Pakistan to stand trial for the September 11 attacks. The deal was that he would be held under house arrest in Peshawar. According to press reports in Pakistan (and the *Daily Telegraph*), this had both bin Laden's approval and that of Mullah Omah, the Taliban leader. The offer was that he would face an international tribunal, which would decide whether to try him or hand him over to America. Either way, he would have been out of Afghanistan, and a tentative justice would be seen to be in progress. . . . Later, a U.S. official said that "casting our objectives too narrowly" risked "a premature collapse of the international effort if by some lucky chance Mr. bin Laden was captured." . . . The "war on terrorism" gave Bush the pretext to pressure Congress into pushing through laws that erode much of the basis of American justice. . . .

In this war between terrorists and the U.S., communications capabilities have been crucial. In an interview with Gen. Mike Hayden (head of the National Security Agency) on CBS' "60 Minutes II" (February 13, 2001, seven months *before* September 11, 2001), Gen. Hayden revealed that "Osama bin Laden has at his disposal the wealth of a $3 trillion-a-year telecommunications industry that he can rely on. . . . He has better technology available to him [than does the NSA]." (It should be remembered here that one of the investors in the Iridium satellite system is the Saudi Binladen Group.) The question is, though, why didn't the NSA pass along all of the relevant information it did have? In Jonathan Landay's article "Agency could have overheard terror dialogue" (*Miami Herald*, June 7, 2002), one learns that

> A secretive U.S. eavesdropping agency monitored telephone conversations before September 11 between the suspected commander of the World Trade Center and Pentagon attacks and the alleged chief hijacker, but did not share the information with other intelligence agencies, U.S. officials said Thursday. The officials, speaking on condition of anonymity, said the conversations between Khalid Shaikh Mohammed and Mohammed Atta were intercepted by the National Security Agency.

Further in this regard, the *Berliner Zeitung* (September 24, 2001) indicated that "experts believe that the suspect [Atta] remained under surveillance in the United States." In the ABC News program "Early Warnings: Pre-Sept. 11 Cautions Went Unheeded," aired February 18, 2002, one also finds out that "ABC News has learned that shortly before Sept. 11, NSA intercepts detected multiple phone calls from Abu Zubaida, bin Laden's chief of operations, to the United States. The intercepts were never passed on."

The excuses for not stopping the attacks of September 11 often include intercepts never being passed on, or that the intercepts didn't arrive in time to be translated before action could be taken. However, the following incident casts some doubt on the validity of this last excuse. According to a report by CBS News on September 4, 2002, it was at 9:53 a.m. on September 11, 2001, that the NSA intercepted a phone call from one of bin Laden's operatives in Afghanistan stating that another target was still to come. Only about two hours later, at 12:05 p.m., the CIA director told Secretary of Defense Donald Rumsfeld about the intercepted conversation. Thus it would seem that the

NSA can translate intercepts rather quickly.

Another question that arises concerning this whole matter is what was the FBI doing, or not doing, with important information? For example, there is an FBI secret document, "Case ID: 199I-WF-213589" (see document on next page). This was reproduced in Greg Palast's *The Best Democracy Money Can Buy* (2002), and he described it as follows:

> FBI confidential. The designation "199" means "national security matter." This is the first of over 30 pages of documentation obtained by the BBC and the National Security News Service [Washington] indicating that the FBI was pulled off the trail of "ABL" [Abdullah bin Laden] on September 11, 1996—and reactivated exactly five years later. According to agents and higher level sources in the CIA who spoke with us, before the attack on the World Trade Center, these cases were shut down for political reasons. While President Clinton "constrained" investigations of alleged Saudi funding of terror networks and the making of the "Islamic" atomic bomb, Bush "Jr." effectively "killed" those investigations—until September 2001.

Noting this, the *Sydney Morning-Herald* (November 7, 2001) published "U.S. agents told: Back off bin Ladens," which begins,

> U.S. special agents were told to back off the bin Laden family and the Saudi royals soon after George Bush became president . . . , it was reported today [on] the BBC2's Newsnight program. . . . A document showed that special agents from the [FBI's] Washington field office were investigating Abdullah, a close relative of Osama, because of his relationship with the World Assembly of Muslim Youth (WAMY), a suspected terrorist organization, it said. . . . The FBI did look into WAMY, but for some reason agents were pulled off the trail, it said.

9/19/01   View Document Text

8:16:52   SECRET   Serial : 39

Case ID. :1991-WF-213589

Responses :

02/23/1996 and closed on 09/11/1996 on ABL because of his
relationship with the WORLD ASSEMBLY OF MUSLIM YOUTH (WAMY), a
suspected terrorist organization.

(S) Investigation to date has determined the following
information: The captioned subject has lived at 850 North Randolph
Street, #1230, Arlington, Virginia 22203 since 08/29/1997. He has
been receiving mail at P.O. Box 8671, Falls Church, Virginia 22041
since 03/11/1996 and may also receive mail at 10310 Main Street,
Fairfax, Virginia 22030. From June 1994 to August 1997, the captioned
subject is believed to have lived with ABL at 3411 Silver Maple
Place, Falls Church, Virgina 22042.

In addition, in the PBS "Frontline" program "The Man Who Knew" (aired October 3, 2002) about FBI counterterrorism chief John O'Neill, the moderator of the program stated: "In 1995, Abdul Hakim Murad told a story of Middle Eastern pilots training at U.S. flight schools, and of a proposal to divebomb a jetliner into a federal building. It was a tantalizing bit of information. [FBI] agents were dispatched, but then withdrawn." The moderator later related that "O'Neill's agents in East Africa had found another training manual nearly identical to the one found in the World Trade Center bombing. One cooperating witness revealed that bin Laden was planning to send operatives to the U.S. for pilot training. A computer found in a raid showed hundreds of targets around the world already surveilled and approved." And still later, the moderator indicated that "an Egyptian informant had told O'Neill and his agents an American warship would be hit by al-Qaeda. Then on October 12, 2000, al-Qaeda struck. The guided missile destroyer *U.S.S. Cole* was the target of a suicide mission." While O'Neill for years had warned those at FBI headquarters about the serious threat posed by al-Qaeda, his appeals for action at some critical times were rejected.

Another incident involving the FBI concerns a Jordanian national, Walid Arkeh. According to *Orlando Sentinel* staff writer Doris Bloodsworth in "Inmate says he told FBI about danger to New York" (January 6, 2002), Arkeh told the FBI on the afternoon of August 21, 2001, that "something big was going to happen in New York City very soon." He said he got the information from "three men who were cronies of bin Laden's," whom federal prosecutors had indicted as co–conspirators with bin Laden in the bombings of U.S. embassies in Kenya and Tanzania, but Florida FBI agents paid little attention to Arkeh's warnings prior to September 11, 2001. When Bloodsworth interviewed him after the attacks ("FBI Gives Terror Tip 2nd Look," *Orlando Sentinel,* October 30, 2002), he told her about what the three terrorists had told him: ". . . A lot of United States government buildings were mentioned, airports, federal buildings" in Washington. "The trade center was mentioned to me. When it got bombed (1993), . . . nothing happened to it. . . . One of the guys said, 'In '93, it wasn't successful. But you can bet on it: It will now.'" After the attacks, Arkeh was taken to New York to talk to FBI agents there. Arkeh said he told them he had called the FBI before the attacks and told them it would be on New York City, and the New York FBI agent replied: "Let me tell you something. If you know what happened in New York, we are all in deep s---. We are in deep trouble."

The American public has also been given the impression that if the FBI had pursued the suggestion from its Phoenix office in the summer of 2001 that Middle Eastern males attending U.S. flight training schools should be investigated, the September 11 attacks could have been avoided. However, the first sentence of the article "FBI Knew Terrorists Were Using Flight Schools" (*Washington Post*, September 23, 2001), explains: "Federal authorities have been aware for years that suspected terrorists with ties to Osama bin Laden were receiving flight training at schools in the United States. . . ." Moreover, the article indicated that FBI agents in 1996 had visited two flight schools where Arabs had received training, to gather information about them. And one of the schools had been attended by Abdul Hakim Murad, upon whose laptop computer found in the Philippines was Project Bojinka, detailing plans to hijack airliners and fly them into the World Trade Center, the Pentagon, and other buildings in the U.S.

Some have argued that the only specific building mentioned in Project Bojinka was the CIA building, and that is why the U.S. government was surprised that the terrorists attacked the World Trade Center and the Pentagon. However, Rafael Garcia III, chairman and CEO of the Mega Group of Computer Companies in the Philippines and the man who decoded Murad's (and Ramzi Youssef's) computer in the Philippines, declared:

Then we found another document that discussed a second alterna-

tive to crash the eleven planes into selected targets in the United
States instead of just blowing them up in the air. These included
the CIA headquarters in Langley, Virginia; the World Trade Center
in New York; the Sears Tower in Chicago; the TransAmerica Tower
in San Francisco; and the White House in Washington, D.C. . . . I
submitted my findings to NBI (National Bureau of Investigation)
officials, who most certainly turned over the report (and the computer) either to then Senator Superintendent Avelino Razon of the
PNP (the Philippine National Police) or to Bob Heafner of the FBI.
. . . I have since had meetings with certain U.S. authorities and they
have confirmed to me that indeed, many things were done in response to my report."

(See Rafael Garcia's "Decoding Bojinka," *Newsbreak Weekly*, November 15, 2001.)

Abdul Hakim Murad was in the Philippines with Ramzi Youssef,
the mastermind behind the first World Trade Center bombing in 1993.
In *Through the Eyes of the Enemy* (1998) by Col. Stanislav Lunev (with
Ira Winkler), this highest ranking military defector from the Soviet
GRU (military counterpart of the KGB) to the U.S. not only described
the existence of Russian suitcase-sized nuclear weapons on U.S. soil,
but he also wrote that "most of the Arab terrorist groups were trained
by the Spetznatz [Soviet Special Forces]. . . . The GRU was responsible for the formation of the terrorist group that [the World Trade
Center bombers] belonged to."

The public has been led to believe that the U.S. had a great lack of
"human intelligence" within the terrorist organizations, and was therefore incapable of knowing what was about to happen on September
11. It's almost as though unless Osama bin Laden telephoned our
intelligence community and told them whom and what he was going
to attack as well as when and how, they couldn't have prevented the
attacks on September 11 from occurring. What our intelligence community did know, however, is revealed in John Diamond's article "U.S.

had agents inside al-Qaeda" (*USA Today*, June 4, 2002), which begins as follows: "U.S. intelligence overheard al-Qaeda operatives discussing a major pending terrorist attack in the weeks before Sept. 11 and had agents inside the terror group." The article later stated:

> Some of the clues lie buried in 350,000 pages of documents turned over by the CIA for the [congressional] hearings: Memos describing al-Qaeda's intent to launch attacks aimed at inflicting heavy casualties in America; reports discussing the possibility of suicide bombings; plots to fly planes into buildings and strikes against the Pentagon, World Trade Center, and other high-profile targets; electronic intercepts as late as Sept. 10 of al-Qaeda members speaking cryptically of a major attack . . . [including] such remarks as . . . "Tomorrow will be a great day for us."

In addition, in Stephen Moss' London *Guardian* (October 10, 2001) interview with Mohammed Heikal (identified as the Arab world's foremost political commentator), Heikal related that "bin Laden has been under surveillance for years: every telephone call was monitored and al-Qaeda has been penetrated by American intelligence, Pakistani intelligence, Saudi intelligence, Egyptian intelligence. They could not have kept secret an operation that required such a degree of organization and sophistication."

Furthermore, we know that Steven Emerson, mentioned earlier, had talked with the FBI and knew years ago that al-Qaeda was in the U.S. (e.g., Boston, Denver, Houston, Tucson, Orlando, and other cities). Bill Gertz, a defense and national security reporter for the *Washington Times* and the author of *Breakdown*, has written about reports on a U.S. intelligence estimate that some five thousand al-Qaeda terrorists are in the U.S. Hasn't the FBI been watching these people? And how did Yossef Bodansky (director of the U.S. House of Representatives Task Force on Terrorism and Unconventional Warfare) know years ago that the Islamist terrorist support system "spanned the

United States" and "included safe houses in major cities, weapons, ammunition, money, systems to provide medical and legal aid, false identity papers, and intelligence for the operative," unless U.S. government agents were monitoring these groups?

In Paul L. Williams' book *Al-Qaeda: Brotherhood of Terror* (2002), this consultant on international terrorism and organized crime for the FBI (for the past seven years) informed that "after the Oklahoma bombing, [Abdul Hakim] Murad told prison guards that [Ramzi] Yousef's 'Liberation Army,' a branch of al-Qaeda, was responsible for it. He later made this same claim in writing." Williams also wrote that

> while making final preparations for [Project] Bojinka, the terrorists met with Terry L. Nichols several times in Cebu City, the Philippines. . . . Some FBI officials now believe that Nichols . . . obtained contact with Yousef through Muslim students at Southwest College [Southwestern Oklahoma State University] in Weatherford, Oklahoma. The officials further believe that Yousef and Murad provided Nichols with training in making and handling bombs. Without such instruction, Nichols and McVeigh would not have been able to assemble a 5,600-pound bomb made of ammonium nitrate and nitromethane. Several informants recently gave testimony that they met Nichols with Yousef in the Philippines and that the American was affectionately known there as "the Farmer."

According to Associated Press writer John Solomon in "Warnings Before 1995 Oklahoma Bombing" (June 20, 2002),

> U.S. intelligence monitored a series of meetings and conferences between senior officials of Iran, Syria, Hezbollah, and other terror organizations in mid-February 1995 in which the subject of killing Americans on U.S. soil came up, officials said. "Iranian sources confirmed Tehran's desire and determination to strike inside the U.S.

against objects symbolizing the American government in the near future," said a Feb. 27, 1995, terror warning by the House Task Force on Terrorism and Unconventional Warfare. The warnings became increasingly specific as to the possible location, type of attack, and likely dates. "These strikes are most likely to occur either in the immediate future or in the new Iranian year—starting 21 March 1995," the congressional task force predicted.

In addition, Jim Crogan in "An Oklahoma Mystery: New hints of links between Timothy McVeigh and Middle Eastern terrorists" (*L.A. Weekly*, July 24–30, 2002) stated that the congressional task force director, Yossef Bodansky,

> writes that after the bombing, it was determined that Oklahoma City had been "on the list of potential targets." . . . An undated intelligence report by Bodansky discusses alleged terrorist training inside the U.S. that included some "Lilly Whites." . . . Bodansky states the training was ordered by Iran and conducted by Hamas operatives. . . . The second training occurred in 1993. It was specifically for Lilly Whites. They also used code names and were given state-of-the-art car-bomb training. Bodansky's sources also report that at least two of the 1993 participants came from Oklahoma City.

Crogan went on to say that former Iraqi soldier Hussain Alhussaini, who some believed could be John Doe No. 2, was working at Boston's Logan Airport (where two of the planes were hijacked on September 11, 2001) at least until 1998, and that "the Massachusetts Port Authority, which oversees Logan's operations, declined to comment on Alhussaini's current work status or his airport duties."

According to Micah Morrison in "The Iraq Connection" (*Wall Street Journal*, September 5, 2002), Alhussaini quit his job at Logan Airport in November 1997, and later told a nurse at a psychiatric clinic: "If anything happens there [World Trade Center], I'll be a suspect."

Morrison went on to say that information developed by KFOR-TV (Oklahoma City) reporter Jayna Davis indicated Alhussaini matched the description of John Doe No. 2, and that Vincent Cannistraro (former CIA official who had once been chief of operations for the agency's counterterrorism center) had received information from a top counterterrorism advisor to the Saudi royal family about a terrorist "squad" possibly (Iraqi) in the U.S. Morrison also wrote that Larry Johnson (former deputy director of the State Department's Office of Counter Terrorism) looked at Jayna Davis' material and concluded that "without a doubt, there's a Middle Eastern tie to the Oklahoma City bombing." And Patrick Lang (former director of the Defense Intelligence Agency's human intelligence collection section) is quoted as having written to Ms. Davis that Alhussaini was likely a member of Unit 999 of the Iraqi Military Intelligence Service, or Estikhabarat, headquartered at Salman Pak southeast of Baghdad, which "deals with clandestine operations at home and abroad."

At last, it appears that some attention is being given to the information compiled by Jayna Davis, as James Patterson in "Congressmen pick up pace of OKC bombing probe" (*Indianapolis Star*, October 12, 2002) wrote that

> Indiana congressman Dan Burton, as chairman of the House of Representatives Committee on Government Reform, continues to push for an explanation of allegations that foreigners were involved in the 1995 Oklahoma City bombing. And during the past week, Sen. Arlen Specter, R-PA, complained to FBI Director Robert Mueller that the FBI and Justice Department were ignoring requests from Specter's staff to answer questions about allegations that Iraqi nationals may have been involved in the April 19, 1995, blast.

Before this article appeared in the *Indianapolis Star*, I had called Rep. Burton's staff and suggested that they attempt to look at the surveillance videos from the front of the Murrah Federal Building to see who John Doe No. 2 was. When I mentioned that the public was not allowed to see the videos because of "national security" reasons (or, legally, because federal judge Richard Matsch had sealed all evidence gathered for Timothy McVeigh's trial), the lead staffer at the time asked why I thought the U.S. government would withhold such videos if they showed Middle Eastern accomplices to the bombing. I replied that such information might be withheld if it showed they were among the eight thousand Iraqi soldiers our government settled here after the 1991 Gulf War, because that would be a serious embarrassment to the government officials who approved and carried out that relocation.

Further along these lines, James Langton writing "Iraqis Linked to Oklahoma atrocity" for the London *Evening Standard* (October 21, 2002) explained that

> senior aides to U.S. Attorney-General John Ashcroft have been given compelling evidence that former Iraqi soldiers were directly involved in the 1995 bombing that killed 185 people. . . . There are serious concerns that a group of Arab men with links to Iraqi intelligence, Palestinian extremists, and possibly al-Qaeda, used McVeigh and Nichols as front men to blow up the Alfred P. Murrah Federal Building in Oklahoma City. . . . [Reporter Jayna Davis] found a brown Chevrolet truck almost identical to that once hunted by the FBI had been seen parked outside the offices of a local property management company several days before the bombing. The owner was a Palestinian with a criminal record and suspected ties to the Palestine Liberation Organization. Later she found that the man had hired a number of former Iraqi soldiers. . . . What increasingly drew Davis' attention was another Iraqi living in Oklahoma City, a restaurant worker called Hussain Hashem Alhussaini, whose photograph was almost a perfect match to the official sketch of "John Doe 2." Alhussaini has a tattoo on his upper left arm, indicating he was once a member of Saddam's elite Republican Guard. . . . Two of the Sep-

tember 11 conspirators held a crucial meeting at a motel in Oklahoma City in August 2001. The motel's owner has since identified them as ringleader Mohammed Atta and Zacarias Moussaoui. . . . The motel is unremarkable—except for one thing. It is where a number of Davis' witnesses are sure they saw McVeigh drinking and perhaps plotting with his Iraqi friends.

Larry Klayman of Judicial Watch, along with attorneys John Michael Johnston and Jay D. Adkisson, have filed a complaint (see website: *www.judicialwatch.org/cases/86/complaint.html*) in the United States District Court for the District of Columbia against the Republic of Iraq seeking compensation on behalf of families of victims in the Oklahoma City bombing. The complaint states that "prior to the Gulf War, Iraq had developed a covert network in the United States to acquire materials for weapons of mass destruction. After the Gulf War, Iraq converted that network into organized terrorist cells. These covert Iraqi procurement and terrorist activities directly involved Oklahoma City, Oklahoma." The cells are probably directed by the Mukhabarat (Iraqi Intelligence Service—IIS, also known as the Department of General Intelligence). The attorneys' complaint also presents evidence that Ramzi Youssef (mastermind of the 1993 World Trade Center bombing) was involved with Terry Nichols in the Oklahoma City bombing, and that Youssef was an Iraqi agent (Youssef first met Nichols in the Philippines on December 17, 1991, not long after the Gulf War). We know that Youssef planned Project Bojinka that called for, among other things, hijacking planes and crashing them into the World Trade Center, the Pentagon, and other places. Thus, if the attacks of September 11 were a fulfillment of Project Bojinka, which was planned by an Iraqi agent (Ramzi Youssef), why hasn't the current Bush administration been making more of this, given that they want to show a connection between Iraq and September 11 in order to justify a war against Iraq? It may be that the administration does not want to call attention to the connection among Youssef, Nichols, the Oklahoma City bombing, and probably some of those eight thousand former Iraqi soldiers mentioned earlier who were settled here by the U.S. government in the first two years of the Clinton administration. This is because this resettlement plan was approved earlier by the State Department under the former President Bush's administration. And if the American public learned of an Iraqi connection to the Oklahoma City bombing, they might say that if the federal government had pursued that connection, the September 11 attacks might have been prevented.

Part II

Returning to the matter of whether the U.S. government had information prior to September 11, 2001, that the terrorist attacks would occur, it has been revealed that such information came from a secret Taliban source. On September 7, 2002, *The Independent* (London) published "Revealed: the Taliban minister, the US envoy, and the warning of September 11 that was ignored" by Kate Clark in Kabul, Afghanistan, in which one learned that

weeks before the terrorist attacks on 11 September, the United States and the United Nations ignored warnings from a secret Taliban emissary that Osama bin Laden was planning a huge attack on American soil. The warnings were delivered by an aide of Wakil Ahmed Muttawakil, the Taliban Foreign Minister at the time, who was known to be deeply unhappy with the foreign militants in Afghanistan, including Arabs. . . . But in a massive failure of intelligence, the message was disregarded. . . . The emissary went first to the Americans, travelling across the border to meet the consul general, David Katz, in the Pakistani border town of Peshawar, in the third week of July 2001. They met in a safehouse belonging to an old mujahedin leader who has confirmed to *The Independent* that the meeting took place. Another US official was also present possibly from the intelligence services. Mr. Katz, who now works at the American embassy in Eritrea, declined to talk about the meeting. . . . Nor did Mr. Katz pass the warning on to the State Department, according to senior US diplomatic sources. When Mr. Muttawakil's emissary returned to Kabul, the Foreign Minister told him to see UN officials. He took the warning to the Kabul offices of the UN-SMA, the political wing of the U.N. These officials heard him out, but again did not report the secret Taliban warning to UN headquarters. . . .

If the American government did have information about the September 11 hijackers before the terrorist attacks, what did they do with it? For example, the *Chicago Tribune* reported on December 13, 2001, that hijacker Ziad Samir Jarrah on January 30, 2001, was detained and questioned by authorities of the United Arab Emirates at the request of the U.S. government. Did the FBI and INS (Immigration and Naturalization Service) receive an alert to watch for him if he entered the U.S.? If not, why not? And according to a *Los Angeles Times* article by Bob Drogin and Eric Lichtblau on September 16, 2001, a U.S. intelligence official said "we videotaped the meeting" in Malaysia in January 2000 of future September 11 hijackers Khalid Almihdhar and Nawaf Alhazmi, members of Osama bin Laden's al-Qaeda terrorist organization.

Concerning this, Bill Gertz in *Breakdown* quoted former Defense Intelligence Agency analyst Kie Fallis as saying:

> I began finding all these relationships between al-Qaeda terrorists and the Iranians, specifically those organizations directly controlled by Iran's Supreme Leader, Ali Khamenei. Al-Qaeda and Iran were also connected to terrorists who belong to the Egyptian Islamic Jihad and the Egyptian Islamic Group. I obtained information in January of 2000 that indicated terrorists were planning two or three major attacks against the United States.

It was in January 2000 that the meeting of al-Qaeda terrorists, including Almihdhar and Alhazmi, took place in Malaysia, and in *Breakdown* Gertz revealed:

What alarmed U.S. intelligence was that Malaysian security officials had traced the men to the Iranian Embassy, where they spent the night. "There are definite connections between al-Qaeda and Iran, namely, the MOIS [Ministry of Intelligence and Security] and the IRGC," one official said. The IRGC is the Iranian Revolutionary Guard Corps, the Islamic shock troops that are key supporters and trainers of international terrorism.

Relevant to al-Qaeda, Iran, and the September 11 hijackers, about four months before the September 11, 2001, terrorist attacks, the official Iranian News Agency (IRNA) published "Cuba and Iran to Fight Jointly the United States" (May 10, 2001), which began with the words: "Iran and Cuba reached the conclusion that together they can tear down the United States." The Cuban connection was also revealed in "Castro's Connection," originally published in the *American Legion* magazine (April 2002). In writing this article, former Marine Corps intelligence officer Paul Crespo related that

> according to an Associated Press report, an Afghan al-Qaeda defector reported seeing Cubans training in camps in the Kunar province of Afghanistan. . . . Following the Sept. 11 attack, [Castro spy Ana Belen] Montes [the senior Cuba analyst at the U.S. Defense Intelligence Agency] allegedly transmitted classified information to her spymasters through Cuba's mission to the United Nations. . . . Martin Arostegui reported in *Insight* that al-Qaeda ringleader Mohammed Atta, who organized the Sept. 11 attacks . . . may have met secretly with Cuban undercover agents shortly after his arrival in the United States last year. Atta's contacts may have also included high-level officials of Cuba's biological warfare program. They allegedly spoke with Atta at a Miami hotel.

Given all of this and Castro's longtime support for anti-American terror groups, it is curious that President George W. Bush did not include Cuba in his "axis of evil." However, it should be remembered that on August 30, 1960, former American ambassador to Cuba Earl E. T. Smith testified to a U.S. Senate Judiciary subcommittee: "The United States Government agencies and the United States press played a major role in bringing Castro to power." (See *Reveille* by Carolyn Fling, who was twice named "Woman of the Year" by Women for Constitutional Government.) Does this mean that President Bush supports Communists like Castro? No, just as one could not say that President Dwight D. Eisenhower supported the Communist Castro when the latter came to power in the late 1950s. However, one should realize that Eisenhower really wasn't running American foreign policy at that time. Rather, it was Council on Foreign Relations (CFR) leaders like Secretary of State John Foster Dulles who were in charge and who allowed Castro to come to power. Similarly, in case the American people have not yet realized it, President George W. Bush is not a towering intellect with tremendous foreign policy experience. Rather, he is being "advised" by power elite CFR members as to what American foreign policy should be regarding Cuba and every other place.

Similar to a plan led by Skull and Bones member William C. Whitney that had certain business interests contributing to both major political parties to control who would be president of the United States, the CFR wants to control who will be the leading Democratic and Republican nominees for president as well. When Vice-President Al Gore seemed to be the clear nominee of the Democratic Party in the presidential race for A.D. 2000, he was invited to become a member of the CFR. However, he refused membership, causing Rush Limbaugh on his national radio program February 25, 1999, to state: "Let me throw something out for you conspiracy believers. . . . Al Gore refused his invitation to join the Council on Foreign Relations. . . . That could be one of the reasons why he's held in some disfavor."

On the other hand, when George W. Bush was thinking about running for president, a leading CFR member, George Shultz (former secretary of state), invited him in April 1998 to a policy discussion at Shultz's home on the Stanford University campus, with other leading CFR members such as Dick Cheney, Paul Wolfowitz, and Condoleezza Rice present. This was the beginning of George W. Bush's training to be president. According to Nicholas Lemann in "Without a Doubt" (*New Yorker,* October 14/21, 2002), "Soon Shultz's experts were being invited to Austin for more seminars. In 1999, Rice resigned as provost at Stanford and became the head of Bush's team of foreign-policy advisors, which was known within the campaign as the Vulcans."

Returning to the information about September 11, 2001, hijackers Almihdhar and Alhazmi, one learns from Michael Isikoff's and Daniel Klaidman's article, "The Hijackers We Let Escape" (*Newsweek,* June 10, 2002) that

> the CIA did nothing with this information. Agency officials didn't tell the INS, which could have turned them away at the border [of the U.S.], nor did they notify the FBI, which could have covertly tracked them to find out their mission. Instead, during the year and nine months after the CIA identified them as terrorists, Alhazmi and Almihdhar lived openly in the U.S. . . . until the morning of September 11. . . . All along, the CIA's Counterterrorism Center— base camp for the agency's war on bin Laden—was sitting on information that could have led federal agents right to the terrorists' doorstep. . . . "There's no question we could have tied all 19 hijackers together," [an FBI] official said.

Apparently, when a CIA agent actually got to Osama bin Laden's "doorstep," the CIA did little with that information either. In Alexandra Richard's October 31, 2001, article ("CIA Agent Allegedly Met bin Laden in July," translated November 1, 2001, by Tiphaine Dickson) in *Le Figaro,* one learns that

Dubai, one of the seven emirates of the Federation of the United Arab Emirates, was the backdrop of a secret meeting between Osama bin Laden and the local CIA agent in July. A partner of the administration of the American hospital in Dubai claims that public enemy number one stayed at this hospital between 4th and 14th July. . . . During the hospital stay, the local CIA agent, known to many in Dubai, was seen taking the main elevator of the hospital to go to bin Laden's hospital room. A few days later, the CIA man bragged to a few friends about having visited bin Laden. Authorized sources say that on July 15th, the day after bin Laden returned to Quetta [Pakistan], the CIA agent was called back to headquarters.

Anthony Sampson in "CIA agent alleged to have met bin Laden in July" (*The Guardian*, November 1, 2001) claimed that "intelligence sources say that another CIA agent was also present." (Remember, this is long after CIA director George Tenet in December 1998 declared that the U.S. is "at war" with Osama bin Laden.) Later in the same article, one learns that after a bin Laden agent was arrested in late July 2001 at the Dubai airport,

according to Arab diplomatic sources as well as French intelligence, very specific information was transmitted to the CIA with respect to terrorist attacks against American interests around the world, including on U.S. soil. A DST [French intelligence agency] report dated 7 September enumerates all the intelligence, and specifies that the order to attack was to come from Afghanistan. . . . Contacts between the CIA and bin Laden began in 1979 when, as a representative of his family's business, bin Laden began recruiting volunteers for the Afghan resistance against the Red Army. . . . In the pursuit of its investigations, the FBI discovered "financing agreements" that the CIA had been developing with its "arab friends" for years. The Dubai meeting is then within the logic of "a certain American policy."

Referring to the final report of the joint congressional committee investigating the attacks of September 11, 2001, James Risen in "Inquiry Is Sharply Critical of Intelligence Agencies for Failing to Prevent Attacks" (*New York Times*, December 12, 2002) noted that

> in June 2001, American intelligence obtained information that indicated that Khalid Shaikh Mohammed, a Kuwaiti extremist, had an active role in sending terrorists to the United States and suggested that he was helping them here, the report said. American intelligence officials have identified Mr. Mohammed as a central planner of 9/11 and is considered one of the most important leaders of al-Qaeda. The report says that before Sept. 11 American intelligence had information that linked Mr. Mohammed to al-Qaeda and to anti-American terrorist plans to use aircraft as weapons.

The director of the CIA at this time (summer 2001) was George Tenet, who had become deputy director in 1995 even though he had never received training as a professional intelligence officer. To be able to do that, one has to have a "mentor" with clout, and George Tenet's was U.S. Senator David Boren, Skull and Bones member and Rhodes Scholar. It was perhaps as a fellow Rhodes Scholar that Boren recommended to president-elect Bill Clinton (Rhodes Scholar) that Tenet be appointed to head the administration's transition team on intelligence. President Clinton would later appoint Tenet as director of the CIA in 1997. President Clinton's first CIA director was James Woolsey (Rhodes Scholar), who is now in the forefront of the effort to have the U.S. attack Iraq. And it was under another Rhodes Scholar, Admiral Stansfield Turner (who had no professional intelligence experience), as director of the CIA on October 31, 1977, that eight hundred twenty positions were cut in the agency's Operations Directorate.

George Tenet was CIA director in 1999 when the federal report, "Sociology and Psychology of Terrorism: Who Becomes a Terrorist and Why?", mentioned in my *September 11 Prior Knowledge,* was released. The report referred to suicide pilots flying hijacked aircraft into the Pentagon, CIA headquarters, or the White House. CBS News' segment "Report Warned of Suicide Hijackings" (May 17, 2002) referring to the report, stated that

> Senator Charles Grassley, a senior member of the Senate Judiciary and Finance committees, demanded the CIA inspector general investigate the report, which he called "one of the most alarming indicators and warning signs of the terrorist plot of Sept. 11." Meanwhile, court transcripts reviewed by the Associated Press show the government had other warning signs between 1999 and 2001 that bin Laden was sending members of his network to be trained as pilots and was considering airlines as a possible target. The court records show the FBI has known since at least 1999 that Ihab Mohammed Ali, who was arrested in Florida and later named as an unindicted co-conspirator in the 1998 U.S. Embassy bombings in Africa, had been sent for pilot training in Oklahoma before working as a pilot for bin Laden.

Early in 2001, Senator Boren, perhaps speaking this time for a fellow member of Skull and Bones, asked president-elect Bush (Skull and Bones member) to keep Tenet as CIA director. According to *Washington Post* reporter Bob Woodward in *Bush at War* (2002), Boren suggested the president-elect ask his father about Tenet, and former President Bush (Skull and Bones member) responded favorably.

On the morning of September 11, 2001, when the planes hit the World Trade Center, George Tenet and David Boren were having breakfast. When he received word of the attack, Tenet told Boren: "This is bin Laden. His fingerprints are all over it." Writing about this in *Breakdown,* Bill Gertz asked: "But if Tenet knew it was bin Laden immediately after the attack, why hadn't the CIA been more alert? Why hadn't it prevented the tragedy?" Further regarding this incident, Bob Woodward in *Bush at War* related that Tenet also had another reaction, one that raised the real possibility that the CIA and the FBI had not done all that could have been done to prevent the terrorist attack. "I wonder," Tenet said, "if it has anything to do with this guy taking pilot training." He was referring to Zacarias Moussaoui, a French citizen of Moroccan descent whom the FBI had detained in Minnesota the previous month after he had acted suspiciously at a local flight training school. Moussaoui's case was very much on his mind. In August, the FBI had asked the CIA and the National Security Agency to run phone traces on any calls Moussaoui had made abroad. He was already the subject of a five-inch-thick file in the bureau.

But the CIA had for some time already suspected that something was going to happen. In Associated Press writer John Solomon's "CIA cited growing risk of attack on U.S. soil in August" (October 4, 2001), he related that an official, speaking only on condition of anonymity, revealed: "There was something specific in early August that said to us that he [bin Laden] was determined in striking on U.S. soil." Relevant to this, Bob Woodward and Dan Eggen in "Aug. Memo Focused on Attacks in U.S." (*Washington Post*, May 18, 2002) begin their article by stating:

> The top-secret briefing memo presented to President Bush on Aug. 6 carried the headline "Bin Laden Determined to Strike in U.S." . . . The document, known as the President's Daily Briefing, underscored that Osama bin Laden and his followers hoped to "bring the fight to America." . . . White House press secretary Ari Fleischer described the briefing as a summary containing "generalized information about hijacking and any number of other things."

This raises the obvious question of why President Bush didn't warn the public that hijacking by terrorists in the U.S. could soon occur.

Concerning the Immigration and Naturalization Service (INS), it also is not entirely without blame when it comes to Muslim terrorists being in the U.S. Hedrick Smith in his PBS program "Should we have spotted the conspiracy?" (January 17, 2002) asked, "How could a handful of young Arabs outsmart the combined forces of the CIA, FBI, and other Western intelligence agencies?" He then said,

> As you see in FRONTLINE's "Inside the Terror Network," there were times when alarm bells should have gone off: The failure of the INS to stop the attack's ringleader, Mohammed Atta, from entering the U.S. three times on a tourist visa in 2001, even though officials knew the visa had expired in 2000 and Atta had violated its terms by taking flight lessons. . . . The FAA's failure to investigate hijackers Mohammed Atta and Marwan al-Shehhi after they abandoned a small plane on a busy taxiway at Miami International Airport in December 2000.

Then on June 22, 2001 (almost three months *before* September 11), *WorldNetDaily* editor Joseph Farah wrote that

> Mexico's National Security Advisor Adolfo Aguilar Zinser made the sensational announcement that Islamic terrorist organizations have a presence along the U.S. border and may be making contacts with Mexican guerrilla groups. . . . Mexican media reports make clear the true purpose of the Islamic terrorists in the country—to carry out guerrilla activities in the United States.

Why hasn't the INS monitored these terrorists more carefully?

But concerning the CIA "sitting on information" as quoted earlier, why would they do that? According to Robert Baer (a CIA agent for over twenty years) in *See No Evil* (2002),

> The CIA was systematically destroyed by political correctness, by petty Beltway wars, by careerism, and much more. . . . Afloat on [a]

sea of self-absorption, the White House and the National Security Council became cathedrals of commerce where the interests of big business outweighed the interests of protecting American citizens at home and abroad. . . . I also looked into reporting on the Saudi royal family.

At this point in Baer's book, CIA censors have blacked out the next eight lines. And in an interview on NBC's "Dateline" on August 25, 2002, Baer commented:

No one in the White House is ready to take on the Saudi royal family. The deliberate blindness came from the top, because the orders were, and they're implicit, do not collect information on Saudi Arabia, because you're going to risk annoying the royal family. Don't even look at it as a conspiracy. It's a consent of silence. The fundamentalists get what they want. The royal family gets what they want. American contractors and business get what they want.

On October 7, 2002, the Council on Foreign Relations (CFR) issued a press release concerning the findings of an independent task force sponsored by the CFR and chaired by Maurice Greenberg, former (now honorary) vice-chairman of the CFR. The task force findings, published in "Terrorist Financing," noted: "For years, individuals and charities based in Saudi Arabia have been the most important source of funds for al-Qaeda. And for years, Saudi officials have turned a blind eye to this problem." It should be remembered here that the Saudi government has funded a radical form of Islam called Wahhabism, of which Osama bin Laden is a follower, and the Saudi royal family has declined to hold a public investigation into whether there are other Saudi conspirators besides the fifteen Saudi al-Qaeda hijackers of September 11, 2001. The CFR press release mentioned above noted: "Confronted with this lack of political will, the task force finds that the Bush administration appears to have made a policy decision not to use the full power of U.S. influence and laws now on the books to pressure other governments to more effectively combat terrorist financing."

Concerning the Bush administration's actions prior to the September 11 attacks, the *St. Petersburg Times* (November 25, 2001) in "Loopholes leave U.S. borders vulnerable" explained that

> under a program called U.S. Visa Express, introduced four months before the September 11 attacks, Saudis were allowed to arrange visas through 10 travel agencies—often without coming to the U.S. Embassy or consulate for interviews. . . . Assistant U.S. Attorney Howard Zlotnick told a magistrate in Las Vegas, "It's no secret that the individuals on Sept. 11 came from Saudi Arabia with visas."

This was long after CIA director George Tenet had informed his deputies that "we are at war" with Osama bin Laden, who was a Saudi (as were fifteen of the September 11 hijackers).

Further pertaining to the Saudis, U.S. Senator Charles Schumer on ABC's "This Week" (November 24, 2002) suggested: "It seems that every time the Saudis are involved, we stop. For months and months and months, the Saudis didn't send us flight manifolds [sic] of who was on their planes—the only country [Saudi Arabia] that was allowed to do that. The Saudis always seem to get a special exception. The administration has to stop this." Two days before this, Michael Isikoff in a *Newsweek* web exclusive (November 22) wrote, "9-11 Hijackers: A Saudi Money Trail?", in which he related that beginning in early 2000, payments were made from an account at Washington's Riggs Bank in the name of Princess Haifa Al-Faisal (wife of Saudi ambassador to the U.S., Prince Bandar bin Sultan, and daughter of the late Saudi King Faisal) to the family of student Omar Al Bayoumi who befriended hijackers Khalid Almihdhar and Nawaf Alhazmi and paid their first two months rent in the U.S. A Saudi official said that the princess made charitable and other donations to many people and could not know where all of the funds would eventually go. Isikoff concluded his web exclusive by stating:

> The leaders of a joint House-Senate Intelligence Committees investigation have vigorously pushed for the release of a classified report that lays out the evidence of the Saudi money flow. But Bush administration officials, led by Attorney General John Ashcroft and FBI Director Robert Mueller, have adamantly refused to declassify the evidence upon which the report is based. Senate Intelligence Committee chairman Sen. Bob Graham declined to discuss the evidence gathered by the joint inquiry, but he said he was upset over the Bush administration's intransigence. "This one stinks of people using classified information" for political purposes, said Graham.

For their part, Saudi officials have proclaimed their innocence when the subject of funding terrorists arises. However, given certain Saudi biases, an investigation is warranted. For example, Niles Latham, in his article "Two Faced" (*New York Post,* December 4, 2002), noted the following:

> "Who committed the events of Sept. 11? . . . I think they [the Zionists] are behind these events," Prince Naif [Saudi interior minister Prince Naif Ibn Abd Al-Aziz] was quoted in a Nov. 29 interview by Kuwait's *Al Siyasa* newspaper. "It is impossible that 19 youths, including 15 Saudis, carried out the operation of Sept. 11," Naif said, adding that "Zionist-controlled media" in the United States is manipulating the terror war to create a backlash against Muslims. Naif is an influential member of the Saudi royal family and is a key defendant in a lawsuit filed by kin of 9/11 victims, who charge him with funneling millions of dollars through charities to Osama bin Laden's network as part of a secret pact to keep al-Qaeda out of Saudi Arabia.

Returning to Robert Baer's *See No Evil* and the subject of American contractors and business, Baer described the activities of Roger Tamraz, who had access to President Clinton. Tamraz had on his payroll people like Senator Edward Kennedy's wife, Victoria, secretary of state Warren Christopher's son, and Lloyd Cutler. Tamraz was interested in oil, and Baer got the impression from Azerbaijani president Heidar Aliyev that "the Clinton administration was pimping for Exxon. . . . [Sheila] Heslin's sole job [at the National Security Council], it seemed, was to carry water for an exclusive club known as the Foreign Oil Companies Group, a cover for a cartel of major petroleum companies doing business in the Caspian." Baer went on to reveal that Heslin's boss, deputy national security advisor Sandy Berger, "headed the interagency committee on Caspian oil policy, which made him in effect the government's ambassador to the cartel. . . . If anyone was going to know just how deeply the major oil companies were into the NSC, it was going to be Don Fowler, [who said] Amoco's ambassador at the NSC [was] Heslin."

Pertaining to Iran, Baer wrote that as he looked at the evidence in front of him,

> the conclusion was unavoidable: The Islamic Republic of Iran had declared a secret war against the United States, and the United States had chosen to ignore it. . . . It was an intelligence report from March 1982—a full thirteen months before the embassy bombing—stating that Iran was in touch with a network capable of destroying the U.S. embassy in Beirut. A subsequent report even specified a date the operation should be carried out.

It was carried out by the Islamic Jihad Organization, which "was merely a front for the Iranians."

One other interesting point raised by Baer in *See No Evil* was in his preface, where he remarked: "The other day a reporter friend told me that one of the highest-ranking CIA officials had said to him, off the record, that when the dust finally clears, Americans will see that September 11 was a triumph for the intelligence community, not a failure." Since I know of no Americans who believe the attacks of September 11, 2001, were a "triumph" of anything good, think about why this high-ranking CIA official would make such a claim. Another strange fact was related by Associated Press writer John Lumpkin in "Agency planned exercise on Sept. 11 built around a plane crashing into a building" (August 21, 2002), which began as follows: "In what the government describes as a bizarre coincidence, one U.S. intelligence agency was planning an exercise last Sept. 11 in which an errant aircraft crashed into one of its buildings. But the cause wasn't terrorism—it was to be a simulated accident." This, however, was not the first such exercise, as Andy Lines (U.S. editor of the British newspaper *The Daily Mirror*) revealed in "Pentagon Chiefs Planned for Jet Attack" (May 24, 2002) that although

> U.S. authorities have consistently claimed they had no idea al-Qaeda was thinking of crashing planes into buildings, [and] President Bush insists no one ever had considered such a devastating attack, military chiefs were so convinced terrorists could fly a plane into the Pentagon that they planned for an attack. Almost 11 months before the September 11 suicide mission killed 189 people at America's defense headquarters, they carried out a detailed emergency exercise.... A report reveals that between October 24 and 26, 2000, military planners held an exercise to prepare for "incidents including a passenger plane crashing into the Pentagon."

Part III

The Bush administration has been trying to demonstrate a connection between the terrorist attacks of September 11 and Iraq, because that would bolster their argument that Saddam Hussein should be removed from power, by military force if necessary. An example of how this has been on the minds of some American government officials for quite some time can be seen in "Plans for Iraq Attack Began on 9/11" (CBS News, September 5, 2002). According to this report, "At 2:40 p.m. [September 11, 2001], the notes [taken by aides to secretary of defense Donald Rumsfeld] quote Rumsfeld as saying he wanted 'best info fast. Judge whether good enough to hit S.H. [Saddam Hussein] at same time. Not only UBL [Usama bin Laden].'"

The Bush administration also warned that Saddam Hussein has weapons of mass destruction. But surely the one way to guarantee that he would use them is to attack Iraq. And although Hussein is evil, surely he knows that if he used such weapons first, he would be committing suicide, as the U.S. would annihilate him. But the American government also has to know that if we attack him, his agents in this country would commence a variety of simple, lethal attacks against Americans everywhere in the U.S. and without the attackers having to commit suicide as did those on September 11, 2001. And in case one thinks there are not enough Iraqis in the U.S. to pose a serious threat, remember that in my *September 11 Prior Knowledge*, I related that the U.S. government had settled eight thousand Iraqi soldiers in our country in 1993–94, and some of them could be Iraqi agents loyal to Saddam Hussein. Plus, Dan Eggen in "Missing Iraqis Sought: FBI

Hunts for Thousands Here Illegally" (*Washington Post*, January 27, 2003) revealed that

> the FBI has launched a concerted search for several thousand illegal Iraqi immigrants who have gone missing while visiting the United States. . . . [Some] who have disappeared from the government's view are more likely to be agents of the Iraqi regime or to be allied with terrorist groups, officials said. . . . A senior U.S. Counterterrorism official [said], "We don't really know how big the problem is or how big the threat might be, but the possibility is real." . . . The missing Iraqis [are] estimated by immigration officials to number 3,000 or more.

Verification for the variety of possible retaliatory actions Saddam might take against the U.S. if he were attacked can be found in "Tracking Saddam's Network" (*U.S. News & World Report*, March 2, 1998) by David E. Kaplan, Bruce B. Auster, and Douglas Pasternak. They interviewed Larry Johnson (deputy director of the State Department's counterterrorism office during the 1991 Gulf War), who said if the U.S. attacks Iraq again, Hussein's retaliation could include car bombs, assassinations, and hostage taking. The authors also wrote that "there is concern that Saddam may turn to weapons of mass destruction. Even poorly delivered chemical or biological agents could provoke panic."

More recent verification of what Saddam might do if attacked can also be found in an October 7, 2002, letter sent from CIA director George Tenet to U.S. Senator Bob Graham, chairman of the Senate Intelligence Committee. The letter states:

> . . . Baghdad for now appears to be drawing a line short of conducting terrorist attacks with conventional or C.B.W. [chemical/biological weapons] against the United States. Should Saddam conclude that a U.S.-led attack could no longer be deterred, he probably would

become much less constrained in adopting terrorist actions. . . . Saddam might decide that the extreme step of assisting Islamist terrorists in conducting a W.M.D. [weapons of mass destruction] attack against the United States would be his last chance to exact vengeance by taking a large number of victims with him. . . .

And in Raleigh, North Carolina, on October 30, former CIA director James Woolsey told WTVD news anchor Steve Daniels that if the U.S. went to war with Iraq, "They might use terrorists to spread biological agents around in the U.S., say, infect people with smallpox, try to get them into the country. This is the great uncertainty about fighting over there, the fact that he [Saddam Hussein] might use weapons of mass destruction."

The *Washington Post* on October 11, 2002, reported that

the House and Senate voted overwhelmingly to grant President Bush the power to attack Iraq unilaterally, remove Saddam Hussein from power and abolish that country's nuclear, chemical and biological weaponry. . . . [But] Rep. Joe Baca voted no after learning in a military briefing this week that U.S. soldiers do not have adequate protection against biological weapons. "As a veteran, that's what hit me the hardest," Baca said. "Would you send someone, knowing they're going to be killed?"

What is curious about the Bush administration's concern that Hussein might use biological or chemical weapons is that in a report titled "U.S. helped Iraq develop bio, chemical arms—report," dated February 13, 1998, from Reuters in London, one learns that

the United States helped Iraq develop its chemical and biological weapons programs in the 1980s . . . Britain's Channel Four television news said. . . . The program said it had found U.S. intelligence documents which showed 14 consignments of biological materials were exported from the United States to Iraq between 1985 and 1989. These included 19 batches of anthrax bacteria. . . . The exports, backed by the State Department, were licensed by the Department of Commerce, it said. . . . No less than 29 batches of material were sent after Iraq had used gas in an attack on the Kurdish town of Halabja in 1988, killing 5,000 people, it said.

Similarly, one reads at the beginning of Patrick E. Tyler's "Officers say U.S. Aided Iraq in War Despite Use of Gas" (*New York Times*, August 18, 2002) that "a covert American program during the Reagan administration provided Iraq with critical battle planning assistance at a time when American intelligence agencies knew that Iraq commanders would employ chemical weapons in waging the decisive battles of the Iran-Iraq war, according to senior military officers with direct knowledge of the program." And during an October 8, 2002, congressional debate over whether to authorize President Bush to use force against Iraq, U.S. Representative Louise Slaughter exclaimed regarding Saddam Hussein: "Sure he has biological weapons. We gave them to him."

What happened was that after our confrontation with Iran over the American hostages they took late in the administration of President Jimmy Carter, the U.S. in the early years of the Reagan administration began making overtures to help Iraq in its conflict with Iran. According to *Washington Post* staff writer Michael Dobbs in his article "U.S. Had Key Role in Iraq Buildup: Trade in Chemical Arms Allowed Despite Their Use on Iranians, Kurds" (December 30, 2002), he revealed that

as part of its opening to Baghdad, the Reagan administration removed Iraq from the State Department terrorism list in February 1982, despite heated objections from Congress. . . . On November 1, 1983, a senior State Department official, Jonathan T. Howe, told Secretary of State George P. Shultz that intelligence reports showed that Iraqi troops were resorting to "almost daily use of CW [chemical warfare]" against the Iranians.

Despite this, on December 20, 1983, Donald Rumsfeld met with Saddam Hussein as a special presidential envoy and, according to Dobbs,

> paved the way for normalization of U.S.-Iraqi relations. Declassified documents show that Rumsfeld traveled to Baghdad at a time when Iraq was using chemical weapons on an "almost daily" basis in defiance of international conventions. . . . The administrations of Ronald Reagan and George H. W. Bush authorized the sale to Iraq of numerous items that had both military and civilian applications, including poisonous chemicals and deadly biological viruses, such as anthrax and bubonic plague.

Commenting on the Rumsfeld trip, Alan Friedman (of the London *Financial Times*) in his book *Spider's Web: The Secret History of How the White House Illegally Armed Iraq* (1993), quoted Howard Teicher (a former National Security Council official who traveled with Rumsfeld to Iraq) as stating: "Here was the U.S. government coming hat-in-hands to Saddam Hussein and saying, 'We respect you, we respect you. How can we help you? Let us help you.'"

The Bush administration has argued that not only does Saddam have weapons of mass destruction, but that he is a threat because he has actually used poison gas against his own people, the Kurds. However, Stephen Pelletiere (author of *Iraq and the International Oil System: Why America Went to War in the Gulf*), who was chief of the Iraq desk at the CIA in the 1980s until 1987, was sent to investigate the gassing of the Kurds in Halabja in 1988 and determined that the allegation against Hussein was a fabrication. It was most likely that the dead Kurds who were found had been killed by Iranian gas, not by the Iraqis. And at the end of the Iran-Iraq war, on September 8, 1988, U.S. Secretary of State George Shultz accused Iraq of gassing Kurds in an area called Amadiyah, although Turkish doctors, the Red Cross and Red Crescent, and the U.N. High Commission for Refugees could not find any victims.

One might also ponder at this point to what extent America's hands are completely clean when it comes to the effects of using chemical and biological agents on its own military forces. Not only were there horrible, lethal consequences to U.S. forces in Vietnam from the use of Agent Orange, but Thom Shanker's "U.S. Troops Were Subjected to a Wider Toxic Testing" (*New York Times*, October 9, 2002) begins with these words: "Acknowledging a much wider testing of toxic weapons on its forces, the Defense Department says it used chemical warfare and live biological agents during cold-war era military exercises on American soil, as well as in Canada and Britain, according to previously secret documents cleared for release to Congress." Later in Shanker's article, one is informed that "in May, the Pentagon disclosed that ships and sailors had been sprayed with chemical and biological agents during cold-war-era testing . . . on the high seas." And he concludes the article by referring

> to claims by veterans that they had suffered health damage from the tests. "The Department of Defense has not only subjected our own soldiers to dangerous substances, it may have put civilians it is charged with protecting at risk," U.S. Representative Mike Thompson said tonight. "It is appalling that 40 years have passed and this information is just now being disclosed."

Of course, the attitude of some government officials has been to keep the experiments on humans secret. On the next page, you can see a declassified letter dated April 17, 1947, from Col. O. G. Haywood, Jr., Corps of Engineers, to a Dr. Fidler with the U.S. Atomic Energy Commission, stating: "It is desired that no document be released which refers to experiments with humans and might have adverse effect on public opinion or result in legal suits. Documents covering such work

Note to Dr. Fidler from O.G. Haywood, Jr. on Medical Experiments on Humans, April 17, 1947.

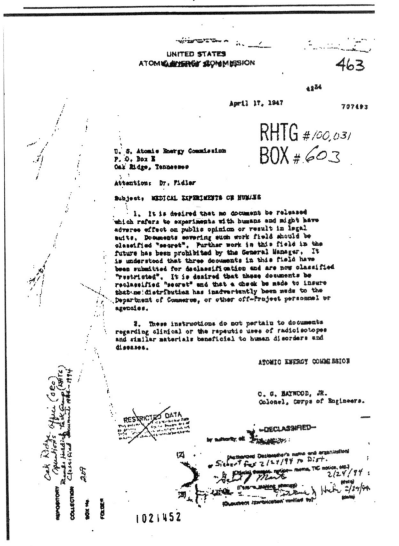

UNITED STATES
ATOMIC ENERGY COMMISSION

463

April 17, 1947

U. S. Atomic Energy Commission
P. O. Box E
Oak Ridge, Tennessee

RHTG #100,031
BOX #603

Attention: Dr. Fidler

Subject: MEDICAL EXPERIMENTS ON HUMANS

1. It is desired that no document be released which refers to experiments with humans and might have adverse effect on public opinion or result in legal suits. Documents covering such work field should be classified "secret". Further work in this field in the future has been prohibited by the General Manager. It is understood that three documents in this field have been submitted for declassification and are now classified "restricted". It is desired that these documents be reclassified "secret" and that a check be made to insure that no distribution has inadvertently been made to the Department of Commerce, or other off-Project personnel or agencies.

2. These instructions do not pertain to documents regarding clinical or therapeutic uses of radioisotopes and similar materials beneficial to human disorders and diseases.

ATOMIC ENERGY COMMISSION

O. G. HAYWOOD, JR.
Colonel, Corps of Engineers.

RESTRICTED DATA

DECLASSIFIED

1021452

field should be classified 'secret.'" In *Breathe No Evil* (1996) by Stephen Quayle and Duncan Long, one learns that in 1995, the U.S. House Government Operations subcommittee on legislation and national security found that between 1940 and 1974, "experiments were performed on possibly as many as a half-million individuals. . . . If this weren't bad enough, it was also discovered that Army researchers sprayed zinc cadmium sulfide—now known to be a carcinogen—over more than 200 cities, apparently to determine how chemical agents might behave in various wind conditions."

But our government's lack of concern for many of our nation's citizens, especially servicemen, has been evident for quite some time. Nearly three thousand American soldiers and sailors died at Pearl Harbor on December 7, 1941, when our government failed to inform them in advance about the Japanese attack there. In John Toland's *Infamy* (1982), he revealed that on December 3, 1941, police lieutenant John A. Burns (who would later be a three-time governor of Hawaii), head of the Honolulu Espionage Bureau, went to the office of Robert L. Shivers, the FBI agent in charge. According to Burns, Shivers said: "Close the doors. I'm not telling my men but I'm telling you this. We're going to be attacked before the week is out," and Pearl Harbor is going to be hit. Toland also revealed that Col. F. G. L. Weijerman, the Netherlands military attaché in Washington, a few days before the Pearl Harbor attack, had taken a message personally to U.S. War Department chief of staff Gen. George C. Marshall that a Japanese fleet was nearing Hawaii. Toland then stated:

> Confirmation of Dutch foreknowledge of the Japanese attack also came from U.S. General Albert C. Wedemeyer. In 1980 he informed the author [Toland] that during a meeting in 1943 Vice Admiral Conrad E. L. Helfrich of the Royal Netherlands Navy expressed wonder that the Americans had been surprised at Pearl Harbor. The Dutch, Helfrich said, had broken the code and knew that the Japanese were going to strike Pearl Harbor. "He seemed surprised that I

did not know this," recalled Wedemeyer. . . "It was his [Helfrich's] clear recollection that his government had notified my government."

Moreover, Toland related that on December 2, 1941, Captain Johan Ranneft, the Dutch naval attaché in Washington was

informed by U.S. Naval Intelligence that two Japanese carriers are proceeding east and are now about halfway between Japan and Hawaii. On December 6 Ranneft again visited the Office of Naval Intelligence and asked where the two Japanese carriers were. An officer put a finger on the wall chart some 300–400 miles northwest of Honolulu. Ranneft reported all this to his ambassador and to his superiors in London.

(See excerpt from Ranneft's diary, below, from the Historical Department of the Netherlands Ministry of Defense.)

2-12-41. Bespreking op Navy Dept, men wijst mij op de kaart de plaats van 2 Japanse carriers uit Japan vertrokken met Oostelijke koers.

3-12-41. Am. vloot te Balik Papan. Duitsland begint te verliezen. Toon dinner Gezant bij in Honor of Secr. of the Navy Knox, aanwezig o.m. Senator Pepper, Walter Lippmann (journalist).

5-12-41. Bespreking op State Dept. van Kurusu en Nomura. Er is een gerucht, dat Am. zal aanvallen in beide gevallen:
1. Japan velt Thai aan.
2. Japan "beschermt" Thqi.

Zaterdag 6-12-41.
Te 0200 's morgens bespreking op Br.Ambassade met Admiral Dan-quast. Hij is juist terug van conferentie op Navy Dept. Men gelooft niet aan directe aanval van Japan nu, uitgezonderd Admiral Turner U.S.N., die een plotselinge Japanse aanval vreest op Manila.
Te 1400 naar Navy Dept., het departement is gesloten behalve de afdeling O.N.I., waar ook nachtwacht zal worden gedaan. Allen aanwezig op O.N.I. spreek Director Adm. Wilkinson, Capt. Mac Collum, LtCdr. Kramer. Krijg nadere gegevens omtrent Japanse eskaderbewegingen in Zuid Chinese Zee, Golf v. Siam. Men wijst mij - op mijn verzoek - de plaats aan van de 2 carriers (zie 2-12-41) beW. Honolulu. Ik vraag, wat het idee is van deze carriers op die plaats waarop geantwoord: vermoedelijk i.v.m. Japanse rapportage bij eventuele Amerikaanse actie Er is niemand van ons, die spreekt over een mogelijke vliegaanval op Honolulu. Ikzelf denk er niet eens over, omdat ik geloof, dat ieder-een te Honolulu 100% on the alert is, zoals iedereen hier op O.N.I. Er heerst op O.N.I. een zeer gespannen stemming.
Te 1600 naar legatie.
's Avonds te 2100 conferentie bij Gezant - aan huis - met Mil Att. Weyerman. Verneem van Gezant, dat President rechtstreeks aan Mikado s einde teneinde conflict te voorkomen. Indien Maandag geen antwoord zou zijn gekomen, wordt toestand hoogst ernstig.
Te 2300 terug naar huis.

Also regarding our government's lack of concern for our service-men, we left American prisoners of war behind in World War I. And at the end of World War II, on March 24, 1945, Averell Harriman (American ambassador to the Soviet Union) cabled President Frank-lin D. Roosevelt:

> Molotov has given me a copy of Stalin's answer to your message regarding American liberated prisoners of war in Poland. . . . We have had continued definite statements . . . that there are no more prisoners left in Poland and each time these statements have been proved to be wrong. . . . When the story of the treatment accorded our liberated prisoners by the Russians leaks out, I cannot help but feel there will be a great and lasting resentment on the part of the American people. . . .

Then two weeks later on April 7 (five days before Roosevelt died), the joint chiefs of staff advised (CM-OUT 64858) that "Russian fail-ure to cooperate in these matters would not be followed by retaliato-ry action on our part at this time." FDR seemed more concerned about the Soviets' participation in the U.N. than in American POWs, and thousands of our soldiers were left behind.

On Dr. Stan Monteith's "Radio Liberty" program for August 1, 2002, author Joseph Douglass, who wrote *Betrayed* (2002), related how the U.S. government knew we had left American soldiers behind after World War II and the Korean and Vietnam wars, and that our government knew the Communists were conducting horrible experi-ments on them, but didn't want the American public to know this. Douglass recounted how one Czech officer in North Korea when they conducted grotesque experiments tried to get some pain medication to our captured soldiers, but he was prevented from doing it. The tortured American soldiers' screaming got so bad, the Czech officer finally committed suicide. And when a North Vietnamese doctor who defected in 1967 tried to tell about the cruel experiments conducted on American prisoners of war in Vietnam, the State Department expressed concern that the American public should not learn how many POWs there were or about the horrible experiments with which they were being tortured. This was at the same time the U.S. helped finance (via credits) the Soviets (who had, along with the North Koreans and North Vietnamese, conducted the experiments) who were building trucks for the North Vietnamese to use in their war against the U.S.

Returning to the confrontation with Iraq today, beyond the question of what weapons Saddam Hussein might use if attacked, there are larger issues. For example, Mark John of Reuters on September 27, 2002, quoted Chinese premier Zhu Rongji as stating, "We have to respect Iraq's sovereignty and territorial integrity. If the weapons inspections do not take place, if we do not have clear proof and if we do not have the authorization of the Security Council, we cannot launch a military attack on Iraq—otherwise, there would be incalculable consequences." Could one of these "incalculable consequences" be China invading Taiwan to preempt the Taiwanese from obtaining their own "weapons of mass destruction"? And if that occurred, how could the U.S. object, especially since our recent presidents have said there is only one China and Taiwan is part of it?

So why is the Bush administration beating the war drums so loudly against Saddam Hussein now? People in the administration say that after the attacks of September 11, 2001, they became concerned that Saddam Hussein might give weapons of mass destruction (WMD) to terrorists. However, we knew long before September 11 that Hussein had WMD, yet we didn't attempt "regime change" by force then. In fact, according to *Washington Post* staff writer Glenn Kessler in "U.S. Decision on Iraq Has Puzzling Past: Opponents of War Wonder When, How Policy Was Set" (January 12, 2003):

> In an interview on NBC's "Meet the Press," about one year before
> the Sept. 11 attacks, [Dick] Cheney defended the decision of George

H. W. Bush's administration not to attack Baghdad because, he said, the United States should not act as though "we were an imperialist power, willy-nilly moving into capitals in that part of the world, taking down governments." In the current environment, he said, "we want to maintain our current posture vis-a-vis Iraq."

And currently, there's no evidence that Saddam Hussein had anything to do with the attacks of September 11.

Some say one of the main reasons the U.S. is so interested in removing Saddam Hussein from power now has to do with oil. You may recall that in my *September 11 Prior Knowledge,* I wrote that in August 1953, CIA director Allen Dulles (who was a CFR president) used a secret ten million dollar fund to have Gen. Norman Schwarzkopf's father train fighters to overthrow the government of Iran when that nation nationalized its oil production. Relevant to this is an example of how the power elite operates. In Pulitzer Prize-winning journalist Ben Bagdikian's *The Media Monopoly,* one learns about

> when Kermit Roosevelt, a former Central Intelligence Agency (CIA) officer, wrote a book called *Countercoup: The Struggle for the Control of Iran.* It was the author's inside version of how intelligence agencies overthrew a left-leaning Iranian premier, Mohammed Mossadegh, in 1953 and reinstated the Shah. The issue was control of oil. The plot was called "Ajax," of which Roosevelt wrote: "The original proposal for Ajax came from the Anglo-Iranian Oil Company (AIOC) after its expulsion from Iran nine months earlier." The book was published by McGraw-Hill in early 1979. Books were on sale in bookstores and reviewer copies were already in the mail when British Petroleum, successor corporation to AIOC, persuaded McGraw-Hill to recall all the books—from the stores and from reviewers.

One might think about this when considering the situation in early 2003 regarding the government of Venezuela and its supply of oil.

Also in 1953, according to Mohammed Haykal's *Cutting the Lion's Tail: Suez Through Egyptian Eyes* (1986), a declassified NSC (National Security Council) document revealed that "United States policy is to keep the sources of oil in the Middle East in American hands." Following this, a 1958 secret British document (File FO 371/132 778) titled "Future Policy in the Persian Gulf" (January 15, 1958), stated that "the major British and other Western interests in the Persian Gulf [are] . . . to defend the area against the brand of Arab nationalism."

"Interests in the Persian Gulf" also were key in the 1991 Gulf War, as Brent Scowcroft in his and President George Bush's book, *A World Transformed* (1998), wrote that "the core of our argument" rested on "preserving the balance of power in the Gulf, opposing unprovoked international aggression, and ensuring that no hostile regional power could hold hostage much of the world's oil supply." In James Chace's "New World Disorder" review of this book in the *New York Times Review of Books* (December 17, 1998), he revealed: "The closest any cabinet member came to acknowledging the heart of the matter was James Baker's press conference in Bermuda on November 13, 1990, when he explained the economic stakes of Iraq's invasion [of Kuwait] for the United States by saying the issue was 'jobs, jobs, jobs.'" And, of course, "jobs" would be lost if the steady flow of oil from the Persian Gulf was disrupted for any length of time because of actions taken by Saddam Hussein.

Concerning today, Frank Viviano in "Energy future rides on U.S. war: Conflict centered in world's oil patch" (*San Francisco Chronicle*, September 26, 2001) remarked that

> the hidden stakes in the war against terrorism can be summed up in a single word: oil. The map of terrorist sanctuaries and targets in the Middle East and Central Asia is also, to an extraordinary degree, the map of the world's principle energy sources in the 21st century. The defense of these energy resources—rather than a sim-

ple confrontation between Islam and the West—will be the primary flash point of global conflict for decades to come, say observers in the region. . . . It is inevitable that the war against terrorism will be seen by many as a war on behalf of America's Chevron, ExxonMobil, and Arco; France's TotalFinaElf; British Petroleum; Royal Dutch Shell, and other multinational giants, which have hundreds of billions of dollars of investment in the region. There is no avoiding such a linkage or the rising tide of anger it will produce in developing nations already convinced they are victims of a conspiratorial collaboration between global capital and U.S. military might.

Similarly, Mo Mowlam (a member of British prime minister Tony Blair's cabinet from 1997 to 2001) in "The real goal is the seizure of Saudi oil" (*The Guardian*, September 5, 2002) wrote:

I keep listening to the words coming from the Bush administration about Iraq and I become increasingly alarmed. . . . The United States can easily contain [Saddam Hussein]. They do not need to try and force him to irrationality. But that is what Bush seems to want to do. Why is he so determined to take the risk? The key country in the Middle East, as far as the Americans are concerned, is Saudi Arabia, the country with the largest oil reserves in the world. . . . It is in the grip of an extreme form of Islam. . . . Since September 11, it has become increasingly apparent to the U.S. administration that the Saudi regime is vulnerable. . . . The possibility of the world's largest oil reserves falling into the hands of an anti-American, militant Islamist government is becoming every more likely—and this is unacceptable. The Americans know they cannot stop such a revolution. They must therefore hope that they can control the Saudi oil fields, if not the government. And what better way to do that than to have a large military force in the field at the time of such disruption. In the name of saving the west, these vital assets could be seized and controlled. . . . If there is chaos in the region, the U.S. armed forces could be seen as a global saviour. Under cover of the war on terrorism, the war to secure oil supplies could be waged. This whole affair has nothing to do with a threat from Iraq—there isn't one. It has nothing to do with the war against terrorism or with morality. Saddam Hussein is obviously an evil man, but when we were selling arms to him to keep the Iranians in check he was the same evil man he is today. He was a pawn then and he is a pawn now. In the same way he served western interests then, he is now the distraction for the sleight of hand to protect the west's supply of oil.

But a war with Iraq would not just be about protecting the west's supply of oil from Saudi Arabia. The vast oil reserves (second largest in the world) of Iraq would also be at stake. If Saddam Hussein's regime were ousted from Iraq, the U.S. would likely have him replaced by Iraqis cooperative with American oil interests, and our military forces would probably remain in Iraq for the foreseeable future to guarantee that "cooperation." The position of the U.S. government would be that our military was remaining for some time in Iraq simply to ensure stability. However, it is highly unlikely that the American government would allow Hussein to be replaced by a similar tyrant opposed to American "national interests." Thus, with the U.S. having a *de facto* control over Iraq's oil, the foreign policy implications would be strategically broad. Focusing on a possible war with Iraq, reporter Deborah Amos on ABC's "Nightline" (October 2, 2002) said: "The future of Iraqi oil is one of the cards that may be on the table with allies France and Russia." She then asked former CIA director (under President Clinton) James Woolsey (Rhodes Scholar, like Bill Clinton): "So oil is at the heart of this war [with Iraq]?" And Woolsey replied: "We can make it a tool of helping promote far more positive French and Russian behavior than we've seen so far. In that sense, yes."

And the oil of Saudi Arabia and Iraq is not all that is at stake, but rather the oil of the entire Caspian Sea area. According to George Monbiot's "A discreet deal in the pipeline" (*The Guardian*, February 15, 2001):

> During the 1999 Balkans war, some of the critics of NATO's intervention alleged that the western powers were seeking to secure a passage for oil from the Caspian Sea. This claim was widely mocked. . . . [However, there is] the Trans-Balkan pipeline, and it's due for approval at the end of next month. Its purpose is to secure a passage for oil from the Caspian Sea . . . passing through Bulgaria, Macedonia, and Albania. . . . In November 1998, Bill Richardson, then U.S. energy secretary, spelt out his policy on the extraction and transport of Caspian oil. "This is about America's energy security," he explained. "It's also about preventing strategic inroads by those who don't share our values. We're trying to move those newly independent countries toward the west. We would like to see them reliant on western commercial and political interests rather than going another way. We've made a substantial political investment in the Caspian, and it's very important to us that both the pipeline map and the politics come out right." . . . On December 9, 1998, the Albanian president attended a meeting about the scheme in Sofia, and linked it inextricably to Kosovo. "It is my personal opinion," he noted, "that no solution confined within Serbian borders will bring lasting peace." The message could scarcely have been blunter: if you want Albanian consent for the Trans-Balkan pipeline, you had better wrest Kosovo out of the hands of the Serbs. In July 1993, a few months before the corridor project was first formally approved, the U.S. sent peacekeeping troops to the Balkans. They were stationed not in the conflict zones in which civilians were being rounded up and killed, but on the northern borders of Macedonia. . . . The pipeline would have been impossible to finance while the Balkans were in turmoil.

And relevant to Afghanistan, in "Yamani: importance of Gulf oil collapses in the interests of the Caspian Sea" (*arabianews.com*, February 1, 2002), one reads that former Saudi oil minister Ahmad Zaki al-Yamani replied to a question on the relation between the war in Afghanistan and the competition for the wealth of the Caspian Sea by stating that the "U.S. has a strategic objective which is to control the oil of the Caspian Sea and to end dependence on the oil of the Gulf. . . . Regrettably we help the U.S. to achieve this objective and the role of the Arab oil will be ended ultimately."

The "realpolitik" attitude of American administrations toward Arabs/Moslems and how our government has used them goes back many years. For example, in "Ex-National Security Chief Brzezinski admits: Afghan Islamism Was Made in Washington" (interview with Zbigniew Brzezinski in *Le Nouvel Observateur*, January 15–21, 1998), President Jimmy Carter's national security advisor Brzezinski revealed that

> it was July 3, 1979, that President Carter signed the first directive for secret aid to the opponents of the pro-Soviet regime in Kabul. . . . That secret operation was an excellent idea. It had the effect of drawing the Russians into the Afghan trap. . . . What is most important to the history of the world? The Taliban or the collapse of the Soviet empire? Some stirred-up Moslems or the liberation of Central Europe and the end of the cold war?

As related in my book, *September 11 Prior Knowledge*, one of the reasons the U.S. government wanted to remove the Taliban from power in Afghanistan was that they were obstacles to oil and gas pipeline construction from the Caspian Sea area through Afghanistan. Of possible interest in this regard is that the *New Straits Times* (June 27, 2001) reported that Malaysian prime minister Mahathir Muhammed at the twentieth Al-baraka symposium for Islamic Economics in Kuala Lampur endorsed and recommended the Islamic dinar as the trade

currency with member countries and that the dinar must be in gold.
Think of what might happen if the Islamic oil-producing nations began to require payment from the West in gold. The Islamic mint announced that

> the Islamic Gold Dinar was officially launched on the 7th Novem-
> ber 2001 by Islamic Mint. . . . The Islamic Gold Dinar was the cur-
> rency of the Muslim community from its first years right up to the
> fall of the Osmanli Khalifate, and was ousted precisely by the per-
> sistent infiltration of non-Shari'i money instruments into the Mus-
> lim societies, by those forces wishing to harness the vast wealth of
> the Islamic homelands. Because of the fundamental political conse-
> quences of the introduction of paper money instruments into the
> Ummah, the reintroduction of the gold money can be expected to
> be an equally significant milestone in the changing tides of the world
> economic—hence social—situation.

In case at this point you are thinking it's ridiculous to believe that the
American government would use our military forces to obtain or protect oil supplies, just read Juan Forero's "New Role for U.S. in Columbia: Protecting a Vital Oil Pipeline" (*New York Times,* October 4,
2002) about a new mission for American counterinsurgency forces in
Colombia

> protecting a pipeline that carries crude to an oil-hungry America.
> The 500-mile pipeline, transporting 100,000 barrels of oil a day for
> Occidental Petroleum of Los Angeles, is emerging as a new front in
> the terror war. . . . Occidental is close to the Bush administration
> and has long lobbied for the United States to be more involved in
> the conflict [in Colombia]. According to the Center for Public In-
> tegrity in Washington, the company contributed $1.5 million to
> presidential and congressional campaigns between 1995 and 2000.
> . . . "We see the oil companies leveraging their influence in Wash-

ington to move the United States toward a counterinsurgency policy," said Ted Lewis of Global Exchange.

Occidental is not only close to the Bush administration, but to Al
Gore as well. Former Vice-President Gore has been a close friend of
Occidental's founder, Armand Hammer, who hired the vice-president's
father (U.S. Senator Al Gore, Sr.) as vice-president of Occidental Petroleum. Hammer once received an autographed portrait of Bolshe-
vist leader V. I. Lenin, which said, "To comrade Armand Hammer."
And David Rogers in the *Wall Street Journal* (October 23, 1987) described Al Gore, Jr., as having "an intellect honed by the education of
the ruling elite." Note this acknowledgment in the *Wall Street Journal*
that there is such a thing as "the ruling elite."

Further regarding what would be done for oil, Nigeria is an oil-
producing nation and supports Robert Mugabe, who is head of Zim-
babwe. The United States and Great Britain helped bring Mugabe to
power, and even though he has become internationally notorious for
"ethnic cleansing," the U.S. and Britain have not demanded that he
be brought before the U.N. tribunal as was Yugoslav leader Slobodan
Milosevic.

And don't forget that oil also played a role in our first war with
Iraq in 1991. "Steel on Steel" host John Loeffler's guest on his radio
program November 9, 2002, was Dave Morris, who was working for
Bechtel in Iraq at the time Kuwait was invaded and when the Gulf
War began. Commenting on the part oil played, Morris recounted:

> What was one of the first things taken out by the Desert Storm
> forces was this brand new Petrochemical Complex No. 1 down in
> Basra. . . . Once that oil hit the market, it would very likely bust
> loose OPEC's control, because in the three months or more leading
> to the invasion of Kuwait, OPEC was holding emergency meetings
> one right after another to try to keep control over their producers to
> keep prices artificially high through limited production. So it seems

to me there might well have been an element of the powers-that-be
didn't want the Basra refinery to come on stream, because it could
have been very unsettling, not just to OPEC countries but the clas-
sic "Seven Sisters," so-called major oil companies.

On January 4, 2003, John Loeffler interviewed Neal Adams, eight-
time karate world champion who has previously held a top-secret
clearance with the CIA. Adams is the author of *Terrorism and Oil* (2003),
the first book to take an in-depth look at the oil industry's vulnerabil-
ities to terrorism. Adams has worked in the oil industry in thirty-five
countries, and his heroics were documented in a technical video called
"Kuwait in Flames," which took top awards at the New York Film
Festival in the industrial video category and first place in the 1993
Telly Awards. He has been featured on the BBC and in *Forbes Magazine,* and his book provides information regarding typical terrorist
weapons, oil supply disruptions, transportation choke points, and
many other areas of concern.

Another theory regarding why all the saber rattling against Hussein is our government's concern for the future of Israel. While we
may not see Hussein as directly threatening the U.S. with a nuclear
device, for example, should he obtain one, he could use it against
Israel. To this, one might respond that would also be suicidal on his
part, because Israel has its own nuclear arsenal with which to retali-
ate. However, because Israel is so small, a nuclear device exploding
there could devastate a large segment of its population. And as Hussein gets into the latter years of his life, he may like nothing better
than to go out in a "blaze of glory" (from his perspective) destroying
Israel. But to this, one might reply, "Why doesn't Israel, then, take
preemptive action against Iraq rather than waiting for the U.S. to
attack?" It should be remembered, though, that such action by Israel
would almost guarantee a united response by other Arab/Muslim
nations in the region. That is why Israel didn't respond to Hussein's
Scud missile attacks against it during the 1991 Gulf War.

Relevant to a possible war with Iraq and how that might fit with both Israeli interests and American oil interests, retired Marine colonel Andrew Finlayson addressed the October 2002 meeting of the John Locke Foundation in Raleigh, North Carolina. Finlayson wrote the first Marines' counterterrorism manual, has spent five years in Saudi Arabia, and is currently under contract with the U.S. State Department. He described various scenarios for a war with Iraq, and stated:

> A scenario I find very interesting and one that would definitely benefit Israel, Jordan, and the United States is the formation of a Hashemite nation, which would mean Jordan would take over western Iraq. . . . It would help Israel, because the Palestinians, which now make up about half of the population of the current Jordan, would then become a minority group and be much more easily handled. Strategically, it also would give us a direct route from Israel through Jordan into the center of the Middle East, and allow us to more effectively control Iraqi oil. That's so important. . . . The Iraqis are going to pay for this war. . . . Iraq has huge capacity for exporting oil. . . . The campaign will cost about $30–$50 billion to win this war, paid for by the oil reserves which we will control at the end of the war. . . . The weakening of Iraq is probably the best thing that could happen to the State of Israel, and that's why the State of Israel is very intent on making sure that we have regime change there.

In case you think the idea of establishing a Hashemite nation is farfetched, on July 8, 1996, the Institute for Advanced Strategic and Political Studies published "A Clean Break: A New Strategy for Securing the Realm." It is a report prepared by the institute's "Study Group on a New Israeli Strategy Toward 2000," with study group leader Richard Perle, whose views have some respect in the current Bush administration, and who is vocal in his support for war against Iraq. In this report, one reads that since Iraq's future could effect the strategic balance in the Middle East profoundly, it would be understandable that Israel has an interest in supporting the Hashemites in their efforts to redefine Iraq. . . . The predominantly Shia population of southern Lebanon has been tied for centuries to the Shia leadership in Najf, Iraq rather than Iran. Were the Hashemites to control Iraq, they could use their influence over Najf to help Israel wean the south Lebanese Shia away from Hizballah, Iran, and Syria.

Something most Americans do not know about the Gulf War, but which is important to understand concerning the threats by President George W. Bush to attack Iraq, is that former President Bush actually feared that Hussein would pull his forces out of Kuwait and there would not be a war. According to *Washington Post* reporter Bob Woodward in *Shadow* (1999), President George H. W. Bush in January 1991 met with Secretary of State James A. Baker III, chairman of the Joint Chiefs of Staff Colin Powell, and National Security Advisor Brent Scowcroft. Woodward wrote that after Baker and Powell indicated they should try a negotiated withdrawal of Iraqi forces from Kuwait:

Next Bush and Scowcroft, almost together, jumped on Powell and Baker. "Don't you realize that if he pulls out, it will be impossible for us to stay?" Scowcroft asked. Bush nodded in agreement as Scowcroft spoke. . . . There was no diplomatic victory that could destroy Saddam's army. Looking squarely at his advisors, the president said plainly, "We have to have a war." His words hung in the air as heavily as any he had ever spoken. Scowcroft was aware that this understanding could never be stated publicly or be permitted to leak out. An American president who declared the necessity of war would probably be thrown out of office. Americans are peacemakers, not warmongers.

Perhaps President George W. Bush in 2003 also believes "we have to have a war" with Iraq. Remember, he once said, "My dad plays a big role in my life as a shadow government" (see "The Quiet Dynasty," *Time*, August 7, 2000).

Even Rush Limbaugh on his November 13, 2002, radio program, referring to Saddam Hussein's acceptance of a U.N. resolution allowing inspectors to return, said: "There is going to be a war, and it won't take much to trigger it. . . . You know what I find very suspicious? We've got this big audiotape from Osama bin Laden. The administration says, 'We think it's the guy.' I'm not surprised they'd say that, keeps everybody all ginned up. . . . I, frankly, think he was incinerated back at Tora Bora." Then Rush played President Bush at a press conference saying, "We'll [be] continuing our hunt to chase these people [terrorists] down," and Rush then said:

> If I didn't know better, I'd say the president is urging these guys to make good on their threats [as if he were saying], "Come on, try it again. We're ready for you." It's obvious that the whole terrorist threat is still huge and being kept that way, whether on purpose or not, I don't know. . . . What I can't put my finger on is the timing of this [bin Laden tape] and Saddam supposedly accepting the U.N. resolution. There just has to be some correlation here. I've been so trained in recent years to ferret out liberal deceit that I may have to retrain my gunsights here to see other kinds of deceit.

In a response to a caller on the subject, Rush then said, "This is a deeply entwined, woven web of deceit out there. This is intricate."

Rush has an aversion to considering the Council on Foreign Relation's (CFR's) involvement in anything, because he believes that to be conspiratorial and therefore nonsense. However, it is curious that the Bush administration around the spring of 2002 seemed to develop an intense interest in overthrowing Saddam Hussein. Previously, the administration's focus had been on Osama bin Laden, and while

President Bush did mention Iraq as part of the "axis of evil" in his State of the Union message early in 2002, he did not propose invading the other members of the axis (which strangely did not include the terrorist-sponsoring Cuba). Perhaps it is *not* a coincidence that in March 2002, the CFR's *Foreign Affairs* published "Next Stop Baghdad?" by Kenneth Pollack (former National Security Council Persian Gulf director and CIA analyst, now senior fellow and director of National Security Studies at the CFR). The CFR then published Pollack's *The Threatening Storm: The Case for Invading Iraq*, building on Pollack's "acclaimed" *Foreign Affairs* article.

Washington Post staff writer Glenn Kessler in his January 12, 2003, article, "U.S. Decision on Iraq Has Puzzling Past: Opponents of War Wonder When, How Policy Was Set," indicated that

> six days after the attacks on the World Trade Center and the Pentagon, President Bush signed a $2^1/_2$-page document marked "TOP SECRET" that outlined a plan for going to war with Afghanistan as part of a global campaign against terrorism. Almost as a footnote, the document also directed the Pentagon to begin planning military options for an invasion of Iraq, senior administration officials said. . . . The December 1, 1997, issue of the *Weekly Standard* . . . headlined its cover with a bold directive: "Saddam Must Go: A How-to Guide." Two of the articles were written by current administration officials, including the lead one, by Zalmay M. Khalilzad, now special White House envoy to the Iraqi opposition, and Paul D. Wolfowitz, now deputy defense secretary. . . . In an open letter to President Bill Clinton in early 1998, Wolfowitz, Khalilzad, and eight other people who now hold positions in the Bush administration—including Defense Secretary Donald H. Rumsfeld—urged Clinton to begin "implementing a strategy for removing Saddam's regime from power."

In my *September 11 Prior Knowledge*, I explained that Khalilzad had been an undersecretary of defense in the former President Bush's administration, and then a lobbyist for the Taliban as a paid advisor to UNOCAL, followed by his working for Condoleezza Rice at the National Security Council in the Bush administration where he is also special envoy to Afghanistan. Kessler in his *Washington Post* article then explained that in the period of January–February 2002, "Bush also secretly signed an intelligence order expanding on a previous presidential finding, that directed the CIA to undertake a comprehensive, covert program to topple Hussein, including authority to use lethal force to capture the Iraqi president." What do you think our attitude would be if the head of some other country had ordered a covert program to topple our president and use lethal force to capture him? However, it was not until a month after Kenneth Pollack's *Foreign Affairs* article, mentioned earlier, that President Bush in April 2002, according to Kessler in his *Washington Post* article, "approached [Condoleezza] Rice. It was time to figure out 'what we are doing about Iraq,' he told her, setting in motion a series of meetings by the principals and their deputies. 'I made up my mind that Saddam needs to go,' Bush hinted to a British reporter at the time. 'That's about all I'm willing to share with you.'"

What I found curious at the time of the 1991 Gulf War to remove Iraqi forces from Kuwait was that prior to the allied attack, Saddam Hussein had about seven hundred to eight hundred "guests" (actually hostages) from other nations whom he could have used at strategic sites as "shields" against attack, but he simply released them after a short while! And what is curious about the September 11, 2001, terrorist attacks is the lack of follow-up. Some people have suggested that Osama bin Laden is still a CIA asset. While I have no knowledge that he is, there are questions about his terrorist operation. How is it that someone with all his resources and ability to execute an intricate operation like September 11 (with nineteen terrorists willing to commit suicide) could not even get one additional terrorist in all these months since September 11, 2001, to commit even one simple non-suicidal terrorist act (e.g., passenger train derailment or food contamination) resulting in many lives lost? Wouldn't an operationally independent terrorist mastermind be able to execute such an attack and even others?

Similarly curious is why would Osama bin Laden on September 11, 2001, simply have several planes fly into buildings when he has biological, chemical, and nuclear weapons of mass destruction? In case you think it's farfetched to believe that terrorists could have a nuclear weapon, it is worth considering that in 1997, U.S. General Charles Horner, who commanded Allied Forces in the Gulf War, declared in an address to the War College, "I predict that a nuclear weapon will be exploded on the territory of the U.S. in the next few years." And not long thereafter, Ambassador Robert Gallucci, who engaged in nuclear weapon negotiations with both Iraq and North Korea, and then became dean of the School of Foreign Service at Georgetown University in Washington, D.C., declared that an American city could be destroyed by a nuclear weapon within ten years, saying:

> One of these days, one of these [rogue] governments fabricates one or two nuclear weapons, and gives them to a terrorist group created for this purpose. The group brings one of these bombs into Baltimore by boat, and drives another one up to Pittsburgh. And then the message comes into the White House. "Adjust your policy in the Middle East, or on Tuesday you lose Baltimore, and on Wednesday you lose Pittsburgh." Tuesday comes, and we lose Baltimore. What does the U.S. do?

Specifically concerning Osama bin Laden and nuclear weapons, in Paul L. Williams' new book, *Al-Qaeda: Brotherhood of Terror*, he reveals that

> In August 1998 bin Laden paid £2 million to a middle man in Kazakhstan to make a deal to buy "nuclear suitcases" from former KGB agents. According to Russian and U.S. intelligence sources, bin Lad-

en, along with members of al-Qaeda's Shura Council, met with Chechen Mafia figures (including former KGB agents) in Grozny, Chechnya, where they made the deal to purchase 20 nuclear suitcases. For these weapons, bin Laden paid $30 million in a combination of cash and two types of heroin that had been refined in his laboratories.... "There is no longer much doubt that bin Laden has finally succeeded in his quest for nuclear suicide bombs," said Yossef Bodansky, who headed the Congressional Task Force on Nonconventional Terrorism in Washington, D.C.... After the catastrophe of September 11, 2001, a federal official said, "The question isn't whether bin Laden has nuclear weapons, it's when he will try to use them."

Williams also indicates that al-Qaeda obtained chemical weapons from North Korea and Iraq, that the FBI said Saddam Hussein gave bin Laden anthrax spores, that he received ebola and salmonella from Iraq and the Soviet Union, botulism biotoxin from the Czech Republic, and sarin from Iraq and North Korea.

On September 8, 2002, Scott Ritter, former chief U.N. weapons inspector in Iraq, addressed the Iraqi parliament, stating:

I know that weapons inspectors were used to collect information pertaining to the security of Iraq and its leadership that had nothing to do with the mandate of disarmament and everything to do with facilitating the unilateral policy objectives of those who sought to interfere in the internal politics of Iraq in a matter totally inconsistent with international law and the mandate of the Security Council governing the work of the inspectors. . . . I know that the vast majority of the more than 100 targets bombed by the United States and Great Britain during Desert Fox [a military aggression in December 1998] had nothing to do with weapons production capability, but rather the leadership and security establishments of the government of Iraq and that the precision in which these targets were bombed was due in a large part to the information gathered by weapons inspectors. . . . There are those who . . . will seek to establish deadlines and issue ultimatums and threaten the use of force to compel Iraq to let the inspectors return. . . . Such proposals are doomed to fail, which in fact might be the very objective of those who would be making them, given that war is apparently their final objective, not disarmament or peace. . . . There are those who wish Iraq harm regardless of the circumstances or costs, and many of these currently reside in the government of the United States.

Referring to both Iraq and Israel regarding a war motive for the American government, Pat Buchanan in "The War Party's imperial plans" (*WorldNetDaily,* September 11, 2002) theorized:

Iraq is the key to the Middle East. As long as we occupy Iraq, we are the hegemonic power in the region. After we occupy it, a window of opportunity will open—to attack Syria and Iran before they acquire weapons of mass destruction. This is the vision that enthralls the War Party—"World War IV," as they call it—a series of "cakewalks," short sharp wars on Iraq, Syria, and Iran to eliminate the Islamic terrorist threat to us and Israel for generations.

On September 12, 2002, President George W. Bush went to the U.N. General Assembly to present his case against Iraq. A little publicized part of the president's speech said that the U.S. was rejoining UNESCO because it has been "reformed." No, UNESCO still promotes political correctness. It still collaborates with the U.N. Population Fund, whose primary partner seems to be the International Planned Parenthood Federation. UNESCO still advocates reproductive health services for children, including abortion. For example, UNESCO supports the International Guidelines on HIV/AIDS and Human Rights which specifically calls upon governments to ensure a "right to safe and legal abortion," as well as to legalize "same-sex marriage" and prostitution. And by mid-September 2002, UNESCO had expanded its global reach by adding nine new places to its listing of World Heritage Sites. Don't forget, not long after Congress authorized U.S. membership in UNESCO on July 30, 1946, Milton Eisenhower (President Eisenhower's brother and consultant to presidents Roosevelt, Truman, Johnson, and Nixon) addressed the closing session of the first day's conference on UNESCO at Wichita, Kansas, saying: "One can truly understand UNESCO only if one views it in its historical context [and] viewed in this way it reveals itself as one more step in our halting, painful, but I think very real progress toward a genuine world government." Similarly, UNESCO's first director-general, Sir Julian Huxley (Fabian Socialist) wrote in *UNESCO: Its Purpose and Its Philosophy* (1948): "In its education program it [UNESCO] can stress the ultimate need for world political unity and familiarize all peoples with the implications of the transfer of full sovereignty from separate nations to a world organization . . . political unification in some sort of world government will be required."

President Bush's speech at the U.N. on September 12 was preceded by a speech by U.N. Secretary-General Kofi Annan, who made some rather telling and revealing remarks concerning the globalist perspective when he declared:

All States [nations] have a clear interest, as well as a clear responsibility, to uphold international law and maintain international order. Our founding fathers, the statesmen of 1945 . . . agreeing to exercise sovereignty together. . . . There is no substitute for the unique legitimacy provided by the United Nations. Member States attach importance, great importance in fact, to such legitimacy and to the international rule of law. . . . They are willing to take actions under the authority of the Security Council, which they would not be willing to take without it. . . . Let us all recognize, from now on—in each capital, in every nation, large and small—that the global interest is our national interest.

A major factor in "the global interest" is Communist China, and it seems that it was from China that the September 11, 2001, terrorists got the idea for their attacks. In "Finding the Real Source of Sept. 11" (*Newsmax*, October 17, 2001) by Dr. Alexandr Nemets (consultant to the American Foreign Policy Council) and Dr. Thomas Torda (who has been a consultant with the Office of Naval Intelligence), one reads that

> according to New York-based Shijie ribao (*World Journal*, Oct. 5, 2001) and Japan's *Evening Fuji* (Oct. 4, 2001), Japanese security organs have decided that the Sept. 11 strikes were based, with very high probability, on the ideas presented in the book "Unrestricted Warfare," published in 1999 by China's People's Liberation Army (PLA). This book . . . was written by two PLA air force senior colonels (i.e., brigadier generals), Qiao Liang and Wang Xiangsui. . . . According to the analysis of the Japanese Security Bureau, the book contains "useful recipes" for those who intend to cause maximum harm to a developed nation. These recipes include hijacking of civilian aircraft and transforming them into "flying bombs" for attacking the most important population centers and facilities such as nuclear power plants. . . . In late September 2001, the two authors of "Unrestricted Warfare" issued a statement: "The September 11 strikes showed how vulnerable the U.S. is, despite its military might, and how many weak points the U.S. defense system contains."

My own viewpoint concerning the situation with Iraq is that there are several possibilities. First, it is possible that the current "good cop, bad cop" scenario plays itself out, as President Bush blusters that the U.S. could strike militarily against Iraq to bring about regime change. Or Secretary of State Colin Powell's pronouncement "that simply disarmament of Iraq is the goal" could be pursued via U.N. weapons inspectors. Of course, once you've gone the U.N. route, successful disarmament of Iraq could enhance the U.N.'s desire for world government status, or raise the problem of what to do if the U.S. wants to attack Iraq but the U.N. disapproves. If the U.S. attacks without U.N. approval, then never again could we threaten another nation with the phrase "the international community has spoken," because that nation could reply, "You didn't obey the U.N.'s wishes regarding Iraq." But Saddam Hussein may actually disarm, at least until the U.N. weapons inspectors have left and the oil embargo is lifted. Then he may uncover his weapons of mass destruction programs, or perhaps return them from Libya, Syria, or North Korea if he has temporarily shifted them there or elsewhere.

Secondly, it's possible that Saddam will voluntarily go into exile, despite his knowledge of what happened to the Shah of Iran after we persuaded him to take that course. Thirdly, it's possible that Saddam will be overthrown. It's unlikely, though, that the people of Iraq will do this without the help of the Iraqi military. And the Iraqi military leaders probably already are being monitored by secret assassins assigned by Saddam to kill them and their families at any hint of disloyalty.

Lastly, it's possible that the U.S. and its allies will actually engage Iraq in military conflict. This might occur even without U.N. approval if, for example, an allied plane just "happens" to be shot down by Iraq while patrolling the "no fly" zone there. If a full-scale military conflict does begin, there are two possibilities. If the war is "staged" (as in "war games"), it will be easily won by the U.S. and its allies with relatively few casualties on our part, even from chemical or biological agents. However, if the war is real, then a ruthless dictatorial regime like Saddam's can be expected to do certain things. They won't engage our air force or army in open battle, because they assume their communications systems will be quickly disrupted or eliminated. Their planes will either be scattered or sacrificed on strategic targets in Kuwait, Saudi Arabia, etc. Their tanks will be placed next to civilian houses in populated areas as was done in Kosovo. The Iraqi populace has already been heavily armed by the government, and soldiers will be scattered among urban houses to be sure the civilians, including women and children, use the weapons against allied forces. This last sentence had been included in this book in January 2003, so it was actually no surprise when on February 4, New Zealand's *Sunday Star-Times* published "Iraqi 'Ghost' army awaits U.S. fighters" quoting Lieutenant General Tawfik al-Yassiri as stating: "Those who are betting that Saddam will be defeated quickly are mistaken. Tens of thousands of elite Iraqi forces have spread underground, above ground, in farms, schools, mosques, churches . . . everywhere. They are not in camps or major installations. These units are prepared for city warfare and have the experience for it." The article indicated that Yassiri took part in a 1991 uprising against Saddam and now heads a council of exiled officers. The article also quoted another exiled officer as saying that some of the best trained Iraqi units "are vicious. They were trained in Europe and do not even wear uniforms," making it difficult for American soldiers to even know who they are. Iraq could also use chemical and biological weapons against Israel (hoping to cause Israeli retaliation which will lead other Arabs to join the conflict on Iraq's side) and against our forces in concentrated urban areas in Iraq, as Saddam hasn't cared in the past whether some of his own people have been killed by them either. Iraqi agents and Arab sympathizers around the world will conduct simple, non-suicidal terrorist acts (e.g., passenger train derailments simply using crowbars at night) that could kill millions in allied nations (especially if Iraqi agents in this country already have weapons of mass destruction here), causing widespread panic and economic chaos, etc. In "WHO issues alert on food terrorism," BBC Geneva correspondent Emma Jane Kirby on January 31, 2003, reported that "the World Health Organization [WHO] has warned [in a 45-page booklet entitled "Terrorist Threats to Food"] that terrorist groups could try to contaminate food supplies," citing the incident in Oregon when members of a cult contaminated restaurant salad bars. Couldn't Saddam Hussein's agents in the U.S. do something at least as bad as that? And if it becomes clear to Saddam Hussein that his defeat is imminent, he will "torch" the Iraqi oil fields, which ABC News Pentagon reporter John McWethy on "Nightline" (January 24, 2003) said would be an "environmental and economic disaster." If these types of realistically expected things *don't* happen at the directions of someone who is truly a ruthless dictator, then one might consider the possibility that this whole scenario has been staged by the power elite to further its aim of world control.

An interesting aside here is that if Saddam is removed from power, there will probably be a great deal of international focus and economic assistance with regard to Iraq. Cities such as Basra could be highlighted, and there might be a world conference held there to promote the goals of the New World Order. Perhaps not coincidentally, this is exactly what author H. G. Wells said seventy years ago in *The Shape of Things to Come* (1933). He predicted that the plan for the "Modern World-State" would come out of a future conference in Basra, at which point "Russia is ready to assimilate. Is eager to assimilate." Wells then wrote that although world government "had been plainly coming for some years, although it had been endlessly feared and murmured against, it found no opposition prepared anywhere." Wells followed this with his book *The New World Order* (1939), in which he revealed: "We are living in the end of the sovereign states. . . . In the great struggle to evoke a Westernized World Socialism, contemporary governments may vanish." In the book, Wells then said that after the world government is established, "Countless people . . . will hate the new world order . . . and will die protesting against it." Note what the *Holy Bible* in Revelation 13 foretells about such times.

Part IV

Relevant to the terrorist attacks of September 11, 2001 (it was on September 11, 1683, that the Christians defeated the Muslim army outside the gates of Vienna), while the CIA was keeping valuable information to itself, apparently other nations' intelligence services were trying to warn the U.S. of possible attacks. Nicholas Rufford of the British newspaper *The Sunday Times* in "MI6 warned U.S. of al-Qaeda attacks" (June 9, 2002) revealed that

> MI6 warned the American intelligence services about a plot to hijack aircraft and crash them into buildings two years before the September 11 attacks. Liaison staff at the American embassy in Grosvenor Square in London were passed a secret report by MI6 in 1999 after the intelligence service picked up indications from human intelligence sources (Humint) that Osama bin Laden's followers were planning attacks in which civilian aircraft could be used in "unconventional ways." . . . "The Americans knew of plans to use commercial aircraft in unconventional ways, possibly as flying bombs," said a senior Foreign Office source.

The London *Telegraph* (September 16, 2001) reported that it learned that "two senior experts with Mossad, the Israeli military intelligence service, were sent to Washington in August to alert the CIA and FBI to the existence of a cell of as many as 200 terrorists said to be preparing a big operation." And closer to the September 11 attacks, according to Yuval Dror in *Ha'aretz* (September 28, 2001), "Officials at instant-messaging firm Odigo confirmed today that two employees received text messages warning of an attack on the World Trade Center two hours before terrorists crashed planes into the New York landmarks."

Daniel McGrory in the *London Times* (June 12, 2002) wrote:

> A Moroccan secret service agent says that for two years he successfully infiltrated al-Qaeda before breaking cover last summer to warn his bosses that the terror group was plotting "something spectacular" in New York. . . . [Agent] Hassan Dabou [said] it would be a "large-scale operation in New York in the summer or autumn of 2001." Secret service chiefs are said to have taken seriously the tip from one of its veteran informants and immediately passed on the details to Washington.

John Cooley in "Other unheeded warnings before 9/11?" (*Christian Science Monitor,* May 23, 2002) also referred to the Moroccan secret service agent, and in addition stated that "weeks before the Sept. 11 attacks, Jordan, beyond a doubt, . . . advised U.S. and allied intelligence that Osama bin Laden's al-Qaeda terrorists were preparing airborne terrorist operations in the continental United States."

Even Russian leader Alexander Putin in an interview on MSNBC (September 14, 2001) said: "I ordered my intelligence to warn President Bush in the strongest terms that twenty-five terrorists were getting ready to attack the U.S., including important government buildings like the Pentagon."

Then there is the possibility that other nations passed along intelligence that we don't even know about yet to American officials. For example, in my *September 11 Prior Knowledge,* I indicated that in the British government's indictment of Osama bin Laden, titled "Responsibility for the Terrorist Atrocities in the United States, 11 September 2001," one reads that "in August and early September close associates of bin Laden were warned to return to Afghanistan from other parts of the world by 10 September. Immediately prior to 11 September some known associates of bin Laden were naming the date for action as on or around 11 September." Is it possible that British agents long before September 11, 2001, had infiltrated bin Laden's al-Qaeda terrorist organization? Relevant to this, Frank Gardner, BBC security correspondent, in "Al-Qaeda 'was making dirty bomb'" (January 31, 2003) reported that "British officials have shown the BBC previously undisclosed material [including] secret intelligence from agents sent by Britain into al-Qaeda training camps in Afghanistan. Posing as recruits, they blended in and reported back. . . . Bin Laden now had gained the expertise and possibly the materials to build a crude radioactive bomb." If these British agents had infiltrated al-Qaeda long before September 11, 2001, might that be how they learned the information about "in August and early September" 2001 and "the date for action as on or around 11 September" quoted above from the British indictment? And wouldn't one expect that they would have passed such valuable information along before September 11 to various American government officials?

Fox News on September 18, 2002, reported that

> according to the Senate Intelligence Committee's inquiry, between June of 1998 and spring of 2001, there were at least 17 specific intelligence indicators that Osama bin Laden planned to attack the U.S. homeland. Between March 2001 and September 2001, there were 11 specific intelligence indicators of an imminent attack in the United States. Between December 1994 and September 2001, there were 12 specific intelligence indicators that al-Qaeda was planning to use aircraft to attack U.S. targets, particularly in New York City and Washington, D.C.

From the "Joint Inquiry Staff Statement, Part 1," released on September 18, 2002, one finds that among the intelligence reports received were the following:

- In June 1998, the intelligence community obtained information from several sources that Osama bin Laden was considering attacks in the U.S., including Washington, D.C., and New York. This information was provided to senior U.S. government officials in July 1998.

- In the fall of 1998, the intelligence community received information concerning a bin Laden plot involving aircraft in the New York and Washington, D.C., areas.

- In the spring of 1999, the intelligence community obtained information about a planned bin Laden attack on a U.S. government facility in Washington, D.C.

The "Joint Inquiry Staff Statement, Part 1" indicates that

despite these reports, the intelligence community did not produce any specific assessments of the likelihood that terrorists would use airplanes as weapons. . . . Despite the intelligence available in recent years, our review to date has found no indications that, prior to September 11, analysts in the intelligence community were . . . considering the likelihood that Osama bin Laden, al-Qaeda, or any other terrorist group, would attack the United States or U.S. interests in this way.

In testimony before a U.S. Senate judiciary subcommittee on February 28, 1998, Dale Watson (chief of the international terrorism section, national security division of the FBI) indicated that he was aware of Project Bojinka, and stated that "the FBI has an enhanced capability to track the activities of foreign terrorist organizations maintaining a presence in the United States." He went on to describe the FBI Counterterrorism Center and how the CIA and Secret Service had a presence there. He then remarked, "This multiagency arrangement provides an unprecedented opportunity for information-sharing and real-time intelligence analysis." Given all of this, members of Congress and the American people felt secure from terrorist attacks, but on September 11, 2001, such attacks did occur. Following the attacks, there was an internal reorganization at FBI headquarters, but guess whom FBI director Robert Mueller appointed on December 2, 2001, to serve as the executive assistant director for counterterrorism/ counterintelligence. That's right, Dale Watson!

Why did FBI director Robert Mueller after September 11, 2001, say that the FBI had no indication that terrorists would hijack airplanes to crash into buildings in the U.S.? Even if they had just watched the Fox television network's "The Lone Gunmen" on March 4, 2001 (six months *before* the September 11 attacks), they would have seen the possibility of such an attack. In this program, a small group of government operatives take control of a jetliner, planning to crash it into the World Trade Center as a "terrorist" attack.

And didn't the FBI Minneapolis office convey its suspicions to FBI headquarters concerning Zacarias Moussaoui wanting flight training to perhaps fly into the World Trade Center? And then on August 26, 2001, French intelligence notified FBI headquarters that Moussaoui had ties with al-Qaeda.

After FBI senior agent Coleen Rowley's exposing of the problems with the FBI's handling of the Moussaoui investigation, one would have thought that those mishandling the case would have been severely reprimanded, if not fired. However, Associated Press writer Ted Bridis in "Criticized FBI counsel gets bonus" (*Atlanta Journal-Constitution*, January 10, 2003) revealed that

an FBI supervisor whose headquarters unit refused to approve a pre-Sept. 11 search warrant against Zacarias Moussaoui has won a presidential citation and large cash bonus, incentives that critics say reward incompetence. The FBI's deputy general counsel, Marion "Spike" Bowman, was among nine current and former FBI officials who last month received Presidential Rank Awards. Each award carries a cash bonus of 20 percent to 30 percent of annual salary.

. . . FBI director Robert Mueller recommended him for the award. The decision angered FBI critics who believe Bowman's lawyers improperly rejected a search warrant request by FBI agents in Minnesota investigating Moussaoui in August 2001. . . . U.S. Senator Charles Grassley asked Mueller to explain in writing his decision to nominate Bowman. He told Mueller that Senate testimony by Bowman during a closed Judiciary Committee hearing in July raised serious questions about the competence of lawyers in the unit. U.S. Senator Richard Shelby, the senior Republican on the Intelligence Committee during its investigation of the FBI, complained last month—just days before Bowman won the award—that Bowman's law unit provided "inexcusably confused and inaccurate information" to FBI investigators in Minneapolis during the Moussaoui case. Shelby said in an 84-page report that the FBI unit's advice turned out to be "patently false" and led agents on a "wild goose chase for nearly three weeks." . . . Shelby said the award showed "no accountability for poor performance at the bureau. . . . They continue to reward bad behavior, and the results speak for themselves." The Senate investigation also criticized Bowman's unit for blocking an urgent request on Aug. 29, 2001, by FBI agents in New York who wanted to begin searching for Khalid Almihdhar, one of the hijackers on the American Airlines flight that crashed into the Pentagon.

FBI supervisor Bill Kurtz and agent Kenneth Williams, both of the Phoenix office, also are now well-known for their attempt to have Middle Easterners at U.S. flight schools investigated. However, not much attention has been given by the major American media and press to Chicago FBI agents like Robert G. Wright, Jr., and Barry Carmody. At a press conference sponsored by Judicial Watch at the National Press Club in Washington, D.C., on May 30, 2002, Special Agent Wright read from a "Mission Statement" titled "Fatal Betrayals of the Intelligence Mission" he had written on June 9, 2001, in which he stated:

There is virtually no effort on the part of the FBI's international terrorism unit to neutralize known and suspected terrorists residing within the United States. Unfortunately, more terrorist attacks against American interests coupled with the loss of American lives will have to occur before those in power give this matter the urgent attention it deserves. Realizing more American lives are going to be needlessly lost. . . .

This was over three months *before* the September 11, 2001, attacks.

Wright and fellow Chicago FBI agent Barry Carmody in sworn statements also related that years ago when another FBI agent was asked to record a conversation with a suspect in a terrorist investigation, the other agent refused, saying, "A Muslim does not record another Muslim." Wright had primarily been following terrorists' money laundering via various Islamic "charities" in the U.S.

Writing about the May 30 press conference, UPI chief White House correspondent Nicholas Horrock in "FBI agent: I was stymied in terror probe" (May 30, 2002) said that Special Agent Wright had filed a lawsuit against the FBI and "unknown officials" of the FBI in the U.S. District Court in Washington, D.C. In the lawsuit, Wright stated:

Indeed, there existed a concerted effort on the part of agents conducting counterterrorism intelligence investigations to insulate the subjects of their investigations from criminal investigation and prosecution. The whole motive for this conduct is simple and quite disturbing. These intelligence agents avoided the new and additional work that would be required. . . .

Horrock wrote that the net result, according to the lawsuit, was that "the FBI was merely gathering intelligence so they would know who to arrest when a terrorist attack occurred."

Although FBI director Robert Mueller announced his appreciation of senior agent Coleen Rowley's public declaration of problems with the Moussaoui investigation, Special Agent Wright received a not-so-veiled threat of criminal prosecution if he spoke publicly about the FBI's failures during his investigations. After September 11, 2001, Judicial Watch chairman and general counsel Larry Klayman said that he contacted FBI headquarters to suggest that Special Agent Wright might be helpful in their investigation of the terrorist attacks. However, according to Klayman, Michael Chertoff, head of the FBI criminal division, said: "We've had enough of conspiracy theories. We're not interested in talking with Special Agent Wright."

When Klayman was asked at the May 30, 2002, press conference why he thought his client, Special Agent Wright, was blocked from pursuing terrorists' money laundering in the U.S. before the September 11 attacks, Klayman replied:

> The monies were going through some very powerful U.S. banks with some very powerful interests in the United States. These banks knew or had reason to know that these monies were laundered by terrorists. And there are very significant potential conflicts of interest in both the Clinton and Bush administrations with the country primarily responsible for funding these charities, namely Saudi Arabia. And we have both Clinton and Bush, and in particular this Bush administration, who is as tight with Saudi Arabia as you can get. This president's father [former President Bush] used to stay with the bin Laden family when he would go to Saudi Arabia. . . . That may help explain why the FBI were nervous about getting into this stuff when the rich and powerful of Washington, D.C., are in fact doing business with some of these entities.

One might also remember here that in Peter Allen's article, "Bin Laden's Family Link to Bush," in the London *Daily Mail* (September 24, 2001), one reads that Osama bin Laden's older brother, Salem, and George W. Bush in the 1970s "were founders of the Arbusto Energy oil company in Mr. Bush's home state of Texas."

And remember that in my *September 11 Prior Knowledge* book, it is mentioned that President George W. Bush in his campaign of 2000 had his picture taken with Sami Al-Arian, current president of the National Coalition to Protect Political Freedom (NCPPF) who was arrested February 20, 2003, as the North American leader of the terrorist Palestine Islamic Jihad. Relevant to the NCPPF and Al-Arian, J. Michael Waller in "'Wahhabi Lobby' Takes the Offensive" (*Insight Magazine*, August 5, 2002) wrote:

> The New York-based National Lawyers Guild (NLG)—officially cited as having been created in the 1930s under Josef Stalin as the foremost legal bulwark for the Communist Party U.S.A., its fronts and controlled organizations—. . . leadership runs the day-to-day operations of the NCPPF, founded in the 1960s to provide legal support for domestic terrorist groups such as the Weather Underground, Symbionese Liberation Army, Black Liberation Army, and Puerto Rican Armed Forces of National Liberation. The NCPPF's current president, Sami Al-Arian, has been identified as a leading figure in the Palestinian Islamic Jihad, on the State Department terrorist list.

When Judicial Watch chairman Larry Klayman was asked if he had sought congressional help in the matter of Special Agent Robert Wright and other FBI agents, he responded: "We've been working on this for months, and you can be assured that there are people in Congress who haven't done their jobs either. Congress' newly found interest in just that as well. The hypocrisy of Congress equals that of the Bush administration. . . ."

Also concerning hypocrisy, William Norman Grigg in "Did We Know What Was Coming?" (*The New American*, March 11, 2002) makes an interesting comparison. He wrote that John Walker Lindh (the "American Taliban") knew "in broad terms" that the [September 11] attacks were coming, even though the specific "texture" was not explained to him. For refusing to act to prevent the massacre, Lindh has been charged with conspiracy to murder Americans. In contrast, the FBI and CIA, which had the same intelligence as Lindh, have been rewarded with generous budget increases.

In the same article, Grigg included the following quote about the September 11 attacks from a former FBI official with extensive counter-terrorism experience:

I don't buy the idea that we didn't know what was coming. Within 24 hours [of the attack] the Bureau had about 20 people identified, and photos were sent out to the news media. Obviously this information was available in the files and somebody was sitting on it. . . . There's got to be more to this than we can see—high-level people whose careers are at stake, and don't want the truth coming out. . . . What agenda is someone following? Obviously, people had to know—there had to be people who knew this information was being circulated. People [like the Black Tuesday terrorists] don't just move in and out of the country undetected. If somebody in D.C. is taking this information and burying it—and it's very easy to control things from D.C.—then this problem goes much, much deeper. . . . It's terrible to think this, but this must have been allowed to happen as part of some other agenda.

News that there would be a terrorist attack on the U.S. did not come only from foreign governments, but was circulating among private individuals also. In Jeffrey Scott Shapiro's article "Prior Knowledge of Sept. 11 Not Just Urban Legend" (*Insight Magazine*, September 10, 2002), he related that a Palestinian boy at New Utrecht High School in Brooklyn, New York, on September 6, 2001, stated: "Do you see those two buildings [World Trade Center towers]? They won't be standing there next week." Shapiro then wrote:

According to students, many of their Arab-American peers were seen taking photographs of the crumbling twin towers from New Utrecht on Sept. 11. "Don't you think it's strange so many of them happened to take their cameras to school that particular day?" one student asked me. . . . On Sept. 10, 2001, a sixth grade student of Middle Eastern descent in Jersey City, New Jersey, said something that alarmed his teacher at Martin Luther King, Jr. Elementary School. "Essentially, he warned her to stay away from lower Manhattan because something bad was going to happen."

And toward the end of the article, Shapiro revealed:

On Nov. 9, 2001, my sources informed me that the same boy [at New Utrecht High School] who predicted the attacks told school officials there would be a plane crash on Nov. 12. I decided to inform an FBI agent I knew who told me that without specific information, there was little they could do. Once again, the boy's prophecy came true. Three minutes after American Airlines Flight 587 took off from JKF International Airport to the Dominican Republic, both its engines fell from its wings, dooming the plane to crash. . . . To date, authorities suspect the crash was an accident. I'm not so sure.

Also according to Jeffrey Scott Shapiro, writing for the *Journal News* of New York on October 11, 2001,

A veteran city police detective . . . said investigators have been learning that many people in New York's Arab-American community had heard rumors about the Sept. 11 attacks before they occurred. The officer said the story "had been out on the street," and the number of leads turning up was so "overwhelming" that it was difficult to tell who had heard about the attacks from secondhand sources and who had heard it from someone who may have been a participant.

One might wonder at this point why no Arab-Americans came forward before September 11 to warn other Americans about what was going to occur. Perhaps they felt they may have been treated like Essam Al Ridi, who earlier helped U.S. officials but paid a price for it (see Judith Miller's article, "A Witness Against al-Qaeda Says the U.S. Let Him Down," *New York Times*, June 3, 2002).

The bottom line is that there was enough information available so that someone in a responsible leadership position should have known what was coming. In fact, in Howard Kurtz's article, "The Reluctant Scrutiny of 9/11" (*Washington Post*, February 7, 2002), he asks: "How could we not have known?" Senator Patrick Leahy, chairman of the Senate Judiciary Committee, said in an interview on CNN June 8, 2002: "There was plenty of information available before September 11. I think historians are going to find, tragically, that had it been acted upon, the hijackers could have been stopped." A week before Senator Leahy's remarks, Senator Arlen Specter said: "I don't believe any longer this is a matter of connecting the dots. I think they had a veritable roadmap. And we want to know why they didn't act on it. I think there was a distinct possibility of preventing 9/11." (See "September 11 attacks called avoidable" by Joyce Howard Price, *Washington Times*, June 9, 2002. Also see "Senate Report on Pre-9/11 Failures Tells of Bungling at FBI" by Philip Shenon, *New York Times*, August 28, 2002.) And according to Greg Miller's article, "Congress Fattens Its Dossier on Sept. 11 Intelligence Errors" (*Los Angeles Times*, June 6, 2002), Senator Bob Graham, chairman of the Senate Intelligence Committee, determined that "had one human being or a common group of human beings sat down with all that information, we could have gotten to the hijackers before they flew those four planes either into the World Trade Center, the Pentagon, or the ground of Pennsylvania."

Since Senator Graham believes we had enough information to "have gotten to the hijackers," it would seem only fair to ask if Senator Graham received information before September 11, 2001, that would have prevented the attacks. According to *Palm Beach Post* staff writer John Pacenti in "Intelligence panel hears from Glass—9/11 Hearings" (October 17, 2002):

> Randy Glass testified Wednesday [October 16] before congressional investigators. . . . In August 2001, . . . he reached out to Sen. Bob Graham and U.S. Rep. Robert Wexler. He said he told staffers for both lawmakers that a Pakistani operative working for the Taliban known as R. G. Abbas made three references to imminent plans to attack the World Trade Center during the probe, which ended in June 2001. At one meeting at New York's Tribeca Grill caught on tape, Abbas pointed to the World Trade Center and said, "Those towers are coming down," Glass said. . . . Graham acknowledged at a news conference in Boca Raton last month that Glass had contact with his office before Sept. 11, 2001, about an attack on the World Trade Center.

In Kathy Kiely's "Panel finds that flaws allowed 9/11" (*USA Today*, July 17, 2002), one learns that

> three years to the day before the attacks that leveled the World Trade Center and damaged the Pentagon, U.S. spymasters concluded they must improve surveillance on terrorists or the nation would face a catastrophic assault. . . . The early prophetic account of a meeting on Sept. 11, 1998, among the unidentified U.S. intelligence officials is cited in Congress' first editorial postmortem on September's terror attacks. . . . Sources familiar with the document confirm that it criticizes the CIA, FBI, and National Security Agency for failing to devote enough attention and resources to counterterrorism before the Sept. 11 attacks. . . . "We've had . . . systemic problems in each different agency that participated in the deficiencies . . . that did allow Sept. 11 to happen," said Rep. Saxby Chambliss.

While Congress took over nine months to produce its "first editorial postmortem," FBI director Robert Mueller just weeks before said he was waiting for his inspector general's report before making any final conclusions about blame within his agency for not preventing the September 11 attacks. Isn't it fortunate that the terrorists waited these many months since September 11, 2001, before striking again (especially since Vice-President Dick Cheney not long after the attacks said the next attack could be "even more devastating" than the September 11 attacks), so that Congress and the FBI could get their reports completed determining what went wrong?

At the same time that Congress was finalizing its first editorial postmortem on the September 11 attacks, the Bush administration was issuing warnings about possible new terrorist attacks. Pertaining to this, CBS's national security correspondent David Martin commented, "Right now they're putting out all these warnings to change the subject from what was known prior to September 11 to what is known now." (See "Journalists See an Alarming Trend in Terror Warnings" by Howard Kurtz in the *Washington Post*, May 27, 2002.)

On September 18, 2002, Kristin Breitweiser, co-chairperson of "September 11th Advocates," delivered a statement, "Concerning the Joint 9/11 Inquiry," to the Senate Select Committee on Intelligence and the House Permanent Select Committee on Intelligence, in which she indicated that in 1997 the Project Bojinka plot "resurfaced during the trial of Ramsi Yousef. . . . During the trial, FBI agents testified that 'the plan targeted not only the CIA but other U.S. government buildings in Washington, including the Pentagon.'" She also said that while Project Bojinka's primary objective was to blow up eleven airliners over the Pacific, "in the alternative, several planes were to be hijacked and flown into . . . targets in the U.S. Among the targets mentioned were CIA headquarters, the World Trade Center, the Sears Tower, and the White House."

She recounted that "one FAA circular from late July 2001, noted according to Condoleezza Rice that there was 'no specific target, no

credible info of attack to U.S. civil-aviation interests, but terror groups
are known to be planning and training for hijackings and we ask you
therefore to use caution.'" Breitweiser then suggested that this and
other similar warnings should have

> been made more public. Airport security officials could have gone
> over all the basics, again, of the steps needed to prevent hijackings.
> The policy of allowing passengers to carry razors and knives with
> blades of up to four inches in length certainly could have come un-
> der scrutiny. Indeed, officials could have issued an emergency di-
> rective prohibiting such potential weapons in carry-on bags. Final-
> ly, all selectees under the Computer Assisted Passenger Pre-Screen-
> ing System (CAPPS), and their carry-on luggage and checked bags,
> could have been subjected to additional screening. Apparently, none
> were on September 11th, although internal FAA documents indi-
> cate that CAPPS selected some of the hijackers. And how many vic-
> tims may have thought twice before boarding an aircraft? How many
> victims would have chosen to fly on private planes? . . . Going fur-
> ther, how many vigilant employees would have chosen to immedi-
> ately flee Tower 2 after they witnessed the blazing inferno in Tower
> 1, if only they had known that an al-Qaeda terrorist attack was im-
> minent?

Later in her statement, she pointed out that

> also ignored by U.S. intelligence agencies was the enormous amount
> of trading activity on the Chicago Exchange Board and in overseas
> markets. . . . An attack by al-Qaeda was expected to occur at any
> given moment. And yet, massive amounts of trades occurred on
> American Airlines, United Airlines, reinsurance companies, and
> leaseholders in the World Trade Center and none of our watchdogs
> noticed? Perhaps even more disturbing is the information regard-
> ing Khalid al-Midhar and Nawaf Alhazmi, two of the hijackers. In

late August, the CIA asked the INS to put these two men on a watch-dog list because of their ties to the bombing of the *U.S.S. Cole.* On August 23, 2001, the INS informed the CIA that both men had already slipped into the country. Immediately thereafter, the CIA asked the FBI to find al-Midhar and Alhazmi. Not seemingly a hard task in light of the fact that one of them was listed in the San Diego phone book, the other took out a bank account in his own name, and finally, an FBI informant happened to be their roommate.

According to Susan Schmidt in "9/11 Panel Discusses Informant: FBI Handling of Man Who Lived With Hijackers at Issue" (*Washington Post,* October 11, 2002):

The joint House-Senate intelligence panel . . . questioned an FBI agent who received information from Abdussattar Shaikh, a San Diego man who rented a room in his house in 2000 to Khalid Al-mihdhar and Nawaf Alhazmi, two of the suicide hijackers. . . . [Earlier] Shaikh said he believed the men were seeking an education in this country and that he saw no signs of radical beliefs. At the time, according to government sources, Shaikh was providing information informally to the FBI. . . . The FBI . . . has resisted a request from Congress to bring Shaikh before the intelligence panel to testify.

Under the heading "Were the Terrorists Already Under Surveillance?" in her statement, Kristin Breitweiser noted that

on September 12, 2001, the *New York Times* reported that "federal agents questioned employees at a store in Bangor, Maine, where five Arab men believed to be the hijackers tried to rent cell phones late last week." . . . The article goes on to state, "the men then phoned Bangor airport trying to get a flight to Boston but were told there was no flight that matched their desired departure time, the authorities said. The men then phoned Portland International Jet-

Port, where two of them apparently made reservations for a flight to Boston on Tuesday morning." How would this information be gleaned so quickly? How would the FBI know to visit a store in Bangor, Maine, only *hours* after the attacks? Moreover, how would they know the details of a phone conversation that occurred a week *prior* to the attacks? Were any of the hijackers already under surveillance? . . . Furthermore, on September 12th, the *New York Times* reported that . . . "officials said . . . they prepared biographies of each identified member of the hijack teams and began tracing the recent movements of the men." . . . How were complete biographies of the terrorists and their accomplices created in such short time? Did our intelligence agencies already have open files on these men? Were they already investigating them? Could the attacks of September 11th been prevented? . . . The third plane was able to fly "loop de loops" over Washington, D.C. . . . After circling in this restricted airspace—controlled and protected by the Secret Service who had an open line to the FAA, how is it possible that the plane was then able to crash into the Pentagon? Why was the Pentagon not evacuated? Why was our Air Force so late in its response?

The desire of Kristin Breitweiser and many others who lost loved ones in the attacks of September 11 was to have an independent commission thoroughly investigate the event. Unfortunately, on November 27, 2002, President Bush announced that Henry Kissinger would head the independent ten-member commission. This virtually guaranteed the American public would *not* learn all there is to know about this tragic event, because Kissinger is a globalist government "insider" who would be "sensitive" to the consequences of exposing "too much." On December 13, Kissinger abruptly resigned as chairman of the committee, because he did not want to reveal his list of clients (he has been a consultant to UNOCAL). And on December 16, he was replaced as commission chairman by former New Jersey governor Thomas Kean.

The point to ponder, though, remains, and that is why President Bush chose Kissinger to chair this commission in the first place. This is especially important given that *Washington Post* reporters Bob Woodward and Carl Bernstein in *The Final Days* wrote:

> Kissinger counseled his aides that deviousness was part of their job. . . . He told one of them, "This is not an honorable business conducted by honorable men in an honorable way. Don't assume I'm that way and you shouldn't be." . . . In [Gen. Alexander] Haig's presence, Kissinger referred pointedly to military men as "dumb, stupid animals to be used" as pawns for foreign policy.

In the early 1950s, Kissinger and William F. Buckley, Jr., became good friends shortly after Buckley graduated from Yale University where he was a member of Skull and Bones. Buckley's mentor was Willmoore Kendall (Rhodes Scholar) who, in addition to being an academic professor, worked for the CIA (formerly OSS, Office of Strategic Services). Buckley began working for the CIA in 1951, which was the same year Tom Braden became a high-level CIA official. And in "Ex-Official of CIA Lists Big Grants to Labor Leaders" (*New York Times,* May 8, 1967), one discovers that Braden said he gave as much as two million dollars per year to Jay Lovestone, a founder of the Communist Party U.S.A. and editor of its newspaper, *The Communist.* Shortly after the *New York Times* article was printed, Braden authored "I'm glad the CIA is 'immoral'" (*Saturday Evening Post,* May 20, 1967), about his own experiences in the early 1950s with the CIA and its manipulations abroad.

On the same day (September 18, 2002) that Kristin Breitweiser gave her statement to the congressional select committees, Eleanor Hill (congressional staff director of an inquiry into the September 11, 2001, attacks) delivered a report to Congress, and testified:

> In December 1998, director of Central Intelligence, George Tenet, provided written guidance to his deputies at the CIA, declaring, in

effect, a "war" with bin Laden. . . . In June 1998, the intelligence community obtained information from several sources that bin Laden was considering attacks in the United States, including Washington, D.C., and New York. . . . In August 1998, the intelligence community obtained information that a group of unidentified Arabs planned to fly an explosive-laden plane from a foreign country into the World Trade Center. . . . In September 1998, the intelligence community prepared a memorandum detailing al-Qaeda infrastructure in the United States, including the use of fronts for terrorist activities. . . . In June 2001, the community issued a terrorist threat advisory, warning U.S. government agencies that there was a high probability of an imminent terrorist attack against U.S. interests by Sunni extremists associated with Bin Laden's al-Qaeda organization. . . . A briefing prepared for senior government officials at the beginning of July 2001 contained the following language: "Based on a review of all source reporting over the last five months, we believe that UBL [Usama bin Laden] will launch a significant terrorist attack against U.S. and/or Israeli interests in the coming weeks. The attack will be spectacular and designed to inflict mass casualties against U.S. facilities or interests. Attack preparedness have been made. Attack will occur with little or no warning."

In this same report, according to Ken Guggenheim (*Washington Post*, September 20, 2002), a

New York-based FBI agent had asked headquarters on Aug. 29, 2001, to allow his office to use its "full criminal investigative resources" to find Khalid al-Mihdhar, one of the two hijackers who intelligence agents had identified as attending an al-Qaeda meeting in Malaysia in January 2000. In an e-mail, headquarters denied the request because al-Mihdhar was not under criminal investigation. It cited the "wall" between intelligence and law enforcement. The agent replied: "Someday someone will die—and wall or not—the public will not

understand why we were not more effective and throwing every
resource we had at certain 'problems.'" . . . In March 2000, a cable
from an overseas CIA station noted that al-Hazmi had flown into
Los Angeles on Jan. 15, 2000. The cable was marked "Action required: None, FYI." [Eleanor] Hill said the missed opportunities to
stop al-Hazmi and al-Mihdhar were the result of institutional problems at intelligence agencies, such as the failure of the FBI and CIA
to communicate with each other. . . .

But how does this explanation fit with the February 28, 1998, congressional testimony (mentioned earlier) by Dale Watson of the FBI,
in which he assured Congress that the multiagency arrangement
among the FBI, CIA, and Secret Service "provides an unprecedented
opportunity for information-sharing and real-time intelligence analysis"?

Guggenheim is an Associated Press (AP) writer, and in a separate
article, "FBI Agent Warned About 9/11 Hijacker" for the AP on September 20, 2002, he further wrote that

on Friday [September 20], President Bush reversed course and
backed efforts by many lawmakers to have an independent commission conduct a broader investigation. But Stephen Push, a leader of
a group of Sept. 11 relatives, said Bush's proposal isn't good enough
because it apparently wouldn't include an investigation of the intelligence agencies themselves. "This is disgraceful, what we're learning about intelligence failures, and the White House is trying to
cover it up," he said.

The next day, Dan Eggen and Dana Priest in "FBI Agent Urged Search
for Hijacker" (*Washington Post*, September 21, 2002) further described
the New York-based FBI agent's plea to search for Khalid Almihdhar,

but lawyers in the FBI's National Security Law Unit refused. . . .
The agent responded in a blistering e-mail to headquarters. "Let's

hope the National Security Law Unit will stand behind their decisions then, especially since the biggest threat to us now, UBL [Usama bin Laden], is getting the most 'protection.'" . . . Sally Regenhard, whose firefighter son Christian was killed at the World Trade Center, said yesterday that "these people are guilty of malfeasance. They should be brought up on criminal charges. They are partly responsible for the deaths of 3,000 people." . . . Congressional investigators found that the CIA repeatedly failed to alert the FBI or others to Almihdhar and his possible connections to terror. . . . The CIA didn't know that the National Security Agency had already linked Alhazmi with al-Qaeda. . . . Investigators noted in their report, by January 2001 the CIA knew that Almihdhar and Alhazmi had been in contact with the suspected mastermind of the *Cole* attack in Malaysia. Yet their names were still not added to a watch list, which would have flagged Almihdhar when he tried to return to the United States months later. CIA officials again failed to inform the FBI of the duo's entry into the country, FBI officials said.

On December 11, 2002, the joint congressional committee investigating the terrorist attacks of September 11, 2001, issued its final report, which was very critical of the intelligence community for failing to prevent the attacks. In his minority report for the joint committee, Senator Richard Shelby exclaimed:

The story of Sept. 11 is one replete with failures: to share information, to coordinate with other agencies; to understand the law, follow existing rules and procedures, and use available legal authorities in order to accomplish vital goals; to devote or redirect sufficient resources and personnel to counterterrorism work; to communicate priorities clearly and effectively to IC [intelligence community] components; to take seriously the crucial work of strategic counterterrorism analysis; and most importantly, to rise above parochial bureaucratic interests in the name of protecting the American people from terrorist attack.

Part V

Might some people prior to September 11, 2001, have actually "connected the dots" and known that a terrorist attack was imminent? In Andrew Gumbel's "Bush Did Not Heed Several Warnings of Attacks" (*The Independent*, in London, September 17, 2001), he revealed that

> from late August [2001] onwards . . . security was abruptly heightened at the World Trade Center with the introduction of sniffer dogs and systematic checks on trucks bringing deliveries. No explanation has been given for this measure. Also in late August, Mr. bin Laden boasted in an interview with the London-based newspaper *al-Quds al-Arabi* that he was planning an unprecedentedly large strike against the United States.

Then, two days after the attacks, in Michael Hirsh's "We've Hit the Targets" (*Newsweek*, September 13, 2001), he revealed that

> the state of alert had been high during the past two weeks, and a particularly urgent warning may have been received the night before the attacks, causing some Pentagon brass to cancel a trip. Why that same information was not available to the 266 people who died aboard the four hijacked commercial aircraft may become a hot topic on the [Capitol] Hill.

Unfortunately, it hasn't become a hot topic, and Congress appears to have not even seriously investigated the matter. This raises the ques-

tion of whether they are deliberately avoiding it. In Evan Thomas'
and Mark Hosenball's "Bush: We're at War" (*Newsweek*, September
24, 2001), they wrote: "On Sept. 10, *Newsweek* has learned, a group of
top Pentagon officials suddenly canceled travel plans for the next
morning, apparently because of security concerns." Now, if somebody called you and said there might be a terrorist attack/hijacking at
some vague time in the future and at some unknown place, would
you call your airlines right away and cancel your flight plans for to-
morrow morning? I doubt it. Therefore, for these top Pentagon officials to take that type of action implies they had a specific, credible
warning of an attack/hijacking perhaps for September 11. Is it worth
remembering at this point that in *September 11 Prior Knowledge*, I related that Gen. Mahmud Ahmad (former director-general of Pakistan's
intelligence service, who had one hundred thousand dollars wired to
hijacking leader Mohammed Atta) was referred to as having arrived
in the U.S. on September 4, 2001, and talking with officials at the
Pentagon and CIA for the week prior to the September 11 attacks?
Was this a coincidence?

Is it possible that the top Pentagon officials mentioned above
somehow learned of two key National Security Agency intercepts on
September 10? According to Bill Gertz in *Breakdown*,

> The day before the September 11 attacks, NSA's electronic ears
> picked up two intercepts, both in Arabic, from the al-Qaeda plot-
> ters. The intercepts disclosed that a major attack was set for the
> next day, according to intelligence officials. One of the intercepts
> stated cryptically, "The match begins tomorrow." A second declared,
> "Tomorrow is zero day." The discussions were between terrorists in
> the United States and al-Qaeda operatives abroad.

Further concerning prior knowledge relevant to the September 11
attacks, in "Aftershocks" (*Counterpunch*, September 14, 2001) by Alexander Cockburn (nationally syndicated columnist, who also writes

for *The Nation*) and Jeffrey St. Clair, they revealed "that an internal memo was sent around Goldman Sachs in Tokyo on September 10 advising all employees of a possible terrorist attack. It recommended all employees to avoid any American government buildings." However, if American government buildings were thought to be possible targets, why did it take F-16 fighters forty-three minutes after air traffic controllers lost contact with the airplane that was to fly into the Pentagon before the fighters took off from Langley Air Force Base in northern Virginia, just two minutes before the American Airlines Boeing 767 crashed into the Pentagon? Whenever an airplane is hijacked, the standard operating procedure is for military aircraft to be scrambled right away. On October 26, 1999, when golfer Payne Stewart's Learjet did not respond to an air traffic controller for about four minutes, the controller called the military (he didn't have to get presidential approval), and only sixteen minutes later, an F-16 had reached the Learjet at forty-eight thousand feet. There are two combat-ready squadrons at Andrews Air Force Base just twelve miles from the White House. They could have reached the hijacked airplane that hit the Pentagon long before the crash. Even the F-15s that were scrambled from Otis Air National Guard Base on Cape Cod could have reached the airplane that crashed into the Pentagon in time, because the F-15s can fly at speeds of eighteen hundred seventy-five miles per hour, and Washington, D.C., is only a little more than two hundred miles from New York City. So what were they all waiting for? Moreover, Kyle Hence, writing "Foreknowledge of 9/11" for the Centre for Research on Globalisation in Montreal, asked: "Why did the missile batteries at the Pentagon not respond to the aircraft as it approached its target? The 'specificity of method' warnings and intelligence would surely have led our national security and intelligence apparatus to be sure our defenses would be on the ready. Would they not?"

Not only is the delayed response by American military aircraft to the attacks of September 11 curious, but so too was the intact presence of terrorists' passports. Carol Brouillet of the Women's International League for Peace and Freedom organized a delegation to meet with the staffs of U.S. senators Dianne Feinstein and Barbara Boxer after the September 11 attacks, and Brouillet noted that certain things were "unbelievable—like a passport floating out of the pocket of a hijacker on a domestic flight, from that inferno to the streets of New York." (The September 16, 2001, *Los Angeles Times*, page 3, reported that a hijacker's passport was found just several blocks from the World Trade Center towers. And ABC News in "Terrorist Hunt," September 12, 2001, said "sources identify a hijacker as S. Suqami, a Saudi national on American Airlines Flight 11, whose passport was recovered in the rubble.") Also, if one looks at the FBI's website (*www.fbi.gov/ page2/labfrom9.htm*), there is a picture of an only slightly damaged passport photo of one of the hijackers from the Pennsylvania site, even though Flight 77's magnetic tape cockpit voice recorder was destroyed in the fire!

In the June 1923 edition of the Council on Foreign Relations journal *Foreign Affairs*, Col. Edward M. House (President Woodrow Wilson's chief advisor) wrote that "if war had not come in 1914 in fierce and exaggerated form, the idea of an association of nations would probably have remained dormant, for great reforms seldom materialize except during great upheavals." Similarly, it took the fierce and exaggerated terrorist attacks of September 11 for Americans to accept "reforms" placing in jeopardy our constitutional rights. Some "reforms" are still unfolding, as Eric Schmitt wrote in "Military Role in U.S. Gains Favor" (*New York Times*, July 21, 2002):

> The four-star general [Ralph E. Eberhart] in charge of defending the United States against attack said he would favor changes in existing law to give greater domestic powers to the military to protect the country against terrorist strikes. The Bush administration has directed lawyers in the Departments of Justice and Defense to review the Posse Comitatus Act of 1878 and any other laws that sharply restrict the military's ability to participate in domestic law enforce-

ment. . . . The general said it was also possible that the North American Aerospace Defense Command, known as NORAD, might expand beyond the United States and Canada to include Mexico, or that the United States might form a separate joint defense command with Mexico.

(See relevant articles in the *Toronto Star*, July 7, 1999, and in the *Ottawa Citizen*, January 24, 2001.)

Since the subtitle of my previous book on this subject, *September 11 Prior Knowledge*, was "Waiting for the Next Shoe to Drop," at least a little space should be devoted here to what the "next shoe" might be. Given the heightened security measures now in place at airports, it seems less likely that we'll see a repeat of the exact events of September 11, 2001. Of course, there still could be the crashing of small planes into structures, but what the terrorists may try next is something entirely different. There could be the release of radioactive, chemical, or biological agents in areas of concentrated population for large-scale effects. Or there could be smaller scale attacks, like those recently in Israel, that would cause great unease among the general population here because they would be feared to occur possibly anywhere at any time after that. This would be part of a psychological attack by terrorists which would, in turn, negatively impact our economy (remember the effect of the September 11, 2001, attacks on the airline industry). I do not want to give many specifics because I don't want to give anyone ideas, but there are many, simple, lethal things terrorists could do in the U.S. that would not entail their committing suicide, but that would create panic and chaos across the land. And these also could be the "next shoes" to drop. One specific that I will give is that after September 11, I mentioned to "Steel on Steel" talk show host John Loeffler that the terrorists could attack our rail system. I said that a crowbar from a hardware store might only cost about five dollars, and the terrorists could easily find out train schedules, and where the downhill grades and curves in the tracks are so that torn up rails could derail trains. Then, on Ocober 24, 2002, the FBI issued a warning that al-Qaeda could soon attack the American transportation system, particularly railroads.

It might be worth noting at this point that in my book *The Globalists: The Power Elite Exposed* (2001), I referred to a Dr. Lawrence Dunegan's recounting of a March 20, 1969, speech by Dr. Richard L. Day (national medical director of Planned Parenthood, 1965–1968). According to Dr. Dunegan, Dr. Day announced that in terms of controlling population: "Everything is in place, and nobody can stop us now. . . . This time we're going to do it right." Dr. Dunegan also recounted that Dr. Day pronounced the following things were planned: more airplane and rail accidents, as well as building and bridge collapses, would occur to create an atmosphere of instability; terrorism would be used to make people demand international controls; and economic interdependence would help lessen national sovereignty, as people would become citizens of the world. Does any of this sound familiar concerning recent events?

Part VI

After the attacks of September 11, 2001, federal authorities rounded up hundreds (perhaps over a thousand) Middle Eastern males and "detained" them in prisons for many months. ABC's "Nightline" (December 27, 2002) was able to interview one of these detainees who was imprisoned for over a year, but who was completely innocent of any terrorist activities. He related how many were kept in solitary confinement and were told by federal guards that they would never be released from prison. He said some of the detainees even tried to kill themselves.

The American people were told that such measures taken with regard to these detainees were only being applied to noncitizens. However, on June 13, 2002, the U.S. Justice Department announced that it would not bring terrorist suspect Jose Padilla (an American citizen) before a military tribunal. Rather, the Justice Department had identified this American citizen as an "enemy combatant," which allows a person to be held without trial until the war on terrorism is over (and this war could last indefinitely). This is an infringement upon Americans' constitutional rights, and sets an extremely dangerous precedent for the future. And if, as President Bush has said, "We're at war," then why weren't the men being held at Guantanamo Bay afforded all of the rights of "prisoners of war" under the Geneva Convention? The Associated Press reporting from Geneva on September 7, 2002, indicated that

departing U.N. human rights chief Mary Robinson, in a bleak assessment of the state of human rights, accused governments of hiding behind the war on terrorism to trample civil liberties and crush troublesome opponents. . . . Robinson said the Bush administration set the tone by holding detainees from Afghanistan without charge at the U.S. Navy base at Guantanamo Bay, Cuba.

One of those being held at Guantanamo Bay was Yasser Esam Hamdi, who is also an American citizen, and has been labeled an "enemy combatant" who can be held without trial. (See Gary Solis' article, "Even a 'Bad Man' Has Rights," in the *Washington Post*, June 25, 2002).

As an example of how the U.S. government has treated prisoners at Guantanamo Bay, ABC's "World News Tonight" broadcast on November 19, 2002, what happened to a Pakistani villager, Mohammed Sagheer, who was imprisoned for almost a year. He had simply come to Afghanistan in the summer of 2001 as part of a teaching group when, in the chaos of battle, he was captured by the Northern Alliance and turned over to the U.S. He was taken to Camp X-Ray in Guantanamo Bay and questioned in chains twice a month. He recounted that some Arab prisoners were interrogated three to four hours a day and that a call to prayer brought punishment from his American jailers. He said: "They beat us. They hit us on the head. Grabbed us by the neck. Some people were unconscious and they were taken to hospital." Sagheer was totally innocent of any terrorist activity, but it took U.S. officials almost a year to acknowledge that and free him. And we're just supposed to trust the government when it tells us an American citizen is an "enemy combatant" whose constitutional rights may be infringed upon? Sagheer's family went heavily into debt and didn't even know he was still alive until they received a letter from him just two months ago. ABC News reporter Bob Woodruff then concludes the story by stating: "Sagheer claims the Americans promised him two thousand dollars compensation, but he was given just one hundred dollars by Pakistani officials when he returned. And worst of all, he says, nobody apologized."

Concerning all six hundred fifty detainees from over forty countries being held at Guantanamo Bay, Sergio Vieira de Mello, U.N.
high commissioner for human rights, said in early December 2002
that the suspects should either be tried for terrorism or turned over
to the judicial authorities in their home countries. He stated, "How
long can you keep a person in legal limbo?"

Beyond simply holding detainees from Afghanistan at Guantanamo Bay, the U.S. government has been sending some prisoners to
countries where they could be tortured! Writing for *The Guardian*,
Duncan Campbell in Los Angeles said in "U.S. sends suspects to face
torture" (March 12, 2002):

> The U.S. has been secretly sending prisoners suspected of al-Qaeda
> connections to countries where torture during interrogation is le-
> gal, according to U.S. diplomatic and intelligence sources. Prison-
> ers moved to such countries as Egypt and Jordan can be subjected
> to torture and threats to their families to extract information sought
> by the U.S. in the wake of the September 11 attacks. The normal
> extradition procedures have been bypassed in the transportation of
> dozens of prisoners suspected of terrorist connections, according
> to a report in the *Washington Post*. The suspects have been taken to
> countries where the CIA has close ties with the local intelligence
> services and where torture is permitted. According to the report,
> U.S. intelligence agents have been involved in a number of interro-
> gations. . . . "After September 11, these sorts of movements have
> been occurring all the time," a U.S. diplomat told the *Washington
> Post*. "It allows us to get information from terrorists in a way we
> can't do on U.S. soil." . . . U.S. forces also seized five Algerian and a
> Yemeni in Bosnia on January 19 and flew them to Guantanamo Bay
> after the men were released by the Bosnian supreme court for lack
> of evidence, and despite an injunction from the Bosnian human rights
> chamber that four of them be allowed to remain in the country pend-
> ing further proceedings.

Concerning what might happen to American themselves, in "Camps for Citizens: Ashcroft's Hellish Vision" (*Los Angeles Times,* August 14, 2002), George Washington University professor of constitutional law (and guest on ABC's "Nightline") Jonathan Turley warned:

Atty. Gen. John Ashcroft's announced desire for camps for U.S. citizens he deems to be "enemy combatants" has moved him from merely being a political embarrassment to being a constitutional menace. Ashcroft's plan, disclosed last week but little publicized, would allow him to order the indefinite incarceration of U.S. citizens and summarily strip them of their constitutional rights and access to the courts by declaring them enemy combatants. The proposed camp plan should trigger immediate congressional hearings and reconsideration of Ashcroft's fitness for this important office. Whereas al-Qaeda is a threat to the lives of our citizens, Ashcroft has become a clear and present threat to our liberties. The camp plan was forged at an optimistic time for Ashcroft's small inner circle, which has been carefully watching two test cases to see whether this vision could become a reality. The cases of Jose Padilla and Yaser Esam Hamdi will determine whether U.S. citizens can be held without charges and subject to the arbitrary and unchecked authority of the government. . . . This week, the government refused to comply with a federal judge who ordered that he be given the underlying evidence justifying Hamdi's treatment. The Justice Department has insisted that the judge must simply accept its declaration and cannot interfere with the president's absolute authority in "a time of war." . . . Ashcroft is a catalyst for constitutional devolution, encouraging citizens to accept autocratic rule as their only way of avoiding massive terrorist attacks. His greatest problem has been preserving a level of panic and fear that would induce a free people to surrender the rights so dearly won by their ancestors. . . . Every generation has its test of principle in which people of good faith can no longer remain silent in the face of authoritarian ambition. If we

cannot join together to fight the abomination of American camps,
we have already lost what we are defending.

But the problem goes beyond simply identifying Americans as "enemy combatants" and holding them indefinitely without trial. It's a matter of whether the U.S. government can kill such American citizens without proof of their guilt. On November 3, 2002, the CIA used a "Predator" unmanned reconnaissance plane's missiles in Yemen to kill six suspected al-Qaeda members, one of whom was an American citizen. Writing for Knight Ridder/Tribune, Melvin A. Goodman (a former senior analyst at the CIA) said regarding this action: "The death of a U.S. citizen among the al-Qaeda suspects raises serious legal and judicial issues. . . . The United States and the CIA have taken the life of a U.S. citizen without any evidence and before any trial. This is lawlessness." (See the Raleigh, North Carolina, *News and Observer*, December 6, 2002.)

Of course, the federal government's position is that we are all just supposed to take their word that these individuals really are "enemy combatants." We're supposed to simply trust the government's word on the matter. Historically, however, taking the government's word for something has been proven problematic. For example, NBC News reported on August 28, 2002, that "researchers said they found a Japanese midget submarine sunk more than an hour before the attack on Pearl Harbor, . . . the first physical evidence to back U.S. military assertions that it fired first against Japan in World War II and inflicted the first casualties." The midget submarine was sunk by the destroyer *U.S.S. Ward,* which notified superiors at Pearl Harbor who, apparently, sat around for over an hour and let the Japanese attack occur on December 7, 1941. Thus, the Japanese attack could not have been the complete "surprise" that the government has claimed it was.

More recently regarding whether Americans can always trust their government, for years after the Gulf War, the Pentagon's official position was, "There is no Gulf War illness." However, in a May 25, 1994,

U.S. Senate report, "U.S. Chemical and Biological Warfare-Related Dual-Use Exports to Iraq and Their Possible Impact on the Health Consequences of the Persian Gulf War," Americans later learned that the U.S. government earlier had knowingly exported biological agents such as anthrax, botulinum, clostridium, and perfringens to Iraq. These were Class III pathogens, and during the Gulf War, there was the probability of chemical and biological exposures of our military forces. The report also indicated there were sick and dying Gulf War veterans, and that the disease is communicable. In a July 24, 1997, Pentagon report, it was estimated that "98,900 troops were in the path of a plume of nerve gas unleashed when U.S. combat engineers blew up the Kamasiyah ammunition depot in southern Iraq in March 1991."

And in another example of whether Americans should always trust our government, Dr. Stan Monteith in his *Radio Liberty* newsletter for July 2002 wrote:

Hundreds of millions of doses of contaminated Sabin vaccine [to fight polio] were given before it was discontinued in the United States. . . . According to Dr. John Martin, an internationally known virologist, ten percent of U.S. college students tested during a recent blood drive were infected with the African green monkey virus (in polio vaccines, as the polio virus was grown in African green monkeys' kidney-tissue cultures), . . . and eighty percent of the Attention Deficit Disorder (ADD) children tested showed evidence of viral infection. Is this why the Centers for Disease Control stopped using the Sabin vaccine?

The choice between national security and our right to privacy was raised by Secretary of Defense William Cohen before the Senate Armed Services Committee in February 1999, when he commented:

We need greater intelligence. That means not only foreign-gathered intelligence, but here at home. That is going to put us on a collision course with rights of privacy. . . . How much are we going to demand of our intelligence agencies, [and] how much are we willing to give up in the way of intrusion into our lives? That is a trade-off that is going to have to come.

Then, immediately after the September 11, 2001, terrorist attacks, Michael Hirsh wrote "We've Hit the Targets" for *Newsweek* (September 13, 2001) and quoted a senior intelligence source as saying, "We're going to have to enact laws that some people from the far left and the far right won't like. We have to understand that national security will have to take some precedence over what we have seen as the right to privacy." On the other hand, according to Judith Miller in "Departing Security Official Issues Warning" (*New York Times*, February 23, 2003), President Bush's cybersecurity chief, Richard A. Clarke, after resigning on January 31 exclaimed: "When we sacrifice our civil liberties and privacy rights, the terrorists win because they have gotten us to change the nature of our country. I have never seen one reason to infringe on privacy or civil liberties."

On October 26, 2001, the USA Patriot Act became Public Law 107-58, and Section 802 of this law states that "the term 'domestic terrorism' means activities that (A) involve acts dangerous to human life that are a violation of the criminal laws of the United States or of any State. . . ." This very broad definition could result in many Americans being labeled "terrorists." The definition of "domestic terrorism" under Section 802 also includes "activities that (B) appear to be intended . . . to influence the policy of a government by intimidation or coercion. . . ." So if someone tells government officials to reject the new world order or be voted out of office, can that be considered "intimidation" and therefore a "terrorist" act?

Relevant to national security taking precedence over our right to privacy, in January 2002, Vice-Admiral John Poindexter returned to the federal government to head the Information Awareness Office (IAO) at the Defense Advanced Research Projects Agency (see its

"all-seeing eye" logo above) in response to the September 11 attacks. One should recall that Poindexter was convicted in 1990 for his part in the Iran-Contra affair (the conviction was overturned because of congressional immunity). Shortly after Poindexter took control of the IAO, John Sutherland in "No More Mr. Scrupulous Guy" (*The Guardian*, February 18, 2002) referred to it as "Big Brother Is Watching You." Similarly, on ABC's "This Week" (November 24), U.S. Senator Charles Schumer remarked, "If we need a Big Brother, Poindexter is the last guy on the list that I would choose." Schumer then referred to "qualities that ought to be involved . . . in anything that involves maybe taking away our freedoms, which in this Brave New World of 9/11. . . ." And ten days earlier, on ABC's "Nightline" (November 14), host Ted Koppel referred to the IAO as "an Orwellian title." At about this same time, John Markoff wrote "Pentagon Plans a Computer System That Would Peek at Personal Data of Americans" (*New York Times*, November 9, 2002), and in this article, one learns that

The Pentagon is constructing a computer system that could create a vast electronic dragnet. . . . As the director of the effort, Vice-Adm. John M. Poindexter has described the system in Pentagon documents and in speeches. It will provide intelligence analysts and law enforcement officials with instant access to information from Internet mail and calling records to credit card and banking transactions and travel documents, without a search warrant. . . . "This could be the perfect storm for civil liberties in America," said Marc Rotenberg, director of the Electronic Privacy Information Center in Washington. "The vehicle is the Homeland Security Act, the technology is DARPA, and the agency is the FBI. The outcome is a system of national surveillance of the American public." . . . If deployed, civil libertarians argue, the computer system would rapidly bring a surveillance state.

John Barry's article in *Newsweek* (December 2, 2002) about Poindexter and the Information Awareness Office was titled "Big Brother Is Back."

And in terms of what type of information the government has been and can be gathering on individuals, I described the National Security Agency's "Echelon" eavesdropping system in my book *The Globalists: The Power Elite Exposed* (p. 222). But according to Jim Wilson's "Spying on Us" (*Popular Mechanics*, April 2001), the NSA is now adding "Tempest," which

can secretly read the displays on personal computers, cash registers, and automatic teller machines, from as far as a half mile away. . . . We think you will agree it also creates a real and present threat to our freedom. . . . NSA is said to have perfected Tempest to the point at which it can reconstruct the images that appear on a video display or TV screen.

On the Internet version of this article is also a place to "click on" for the declassified NSA report on "Tempest."

The Homeland Security Act was finally passed by Congress on November 19, 2002, and signed into law by President Bush on November 25. Commenting on this act and the USA Patriot Act, Judge Andrew Napolitano, senior judicial analyst for Fox News, on a November 22 broadcast, remarked:

> Well, if you combine the bill that enacted the Homeland Security Department with the USA Patriot Act, which is now a year old, if you read those two bills together, yes, there is an argument that some have made that this is Big Brother come to life. . . . Do we trust this power in the hands of George Bush's predecessor or his successor, if she has the same name as his predecessor?

On June 7, 2002, John Dean (counselor to President Richard Nixon) referred to America sliding into a "constitutional dictatorship," and on July 20 the *Detroit Free Press* published a story ("Arabs in U.S. could be held, official warns") referring to a member of the U.S. Civil Rights Commission speaking of the possibility of internment camps for Arab-Americans. From where did this idea of internment camps for Americans come? Ritt Goldstein in "Foundations are in place for martial law in the U.S." (*Sydney Morning-Herald,* July 27, 2002) wrote that "from 1982–84 Colonel Oliver North assisted FEMA in drafting its civil defense preparations. Details . . . included executive orders providing for suspension of the Constitution, the imposition of martial law, internment camps, and the turning over of government to the president and FEMA."

In case one thinks Goldstein is just imagining things, there is a videotape of U.S. Rep. Jack Brooks during the Iran-Contra hearings questioning Colonel North about his work for the National Security Council. Brooks states: "I read in several papers that there had been developed a contingency plan, in the event of an emergency, by that same agency [NSC] that would suspend the American Constitution." U.S. Senator Daniel Inouye then interrupts Rep. Brooks saying this was a "highly sensitive area" and requested "that that matter not be touched upon at this stage." U.S. Rep. Henry Gonzalez later commenting on this on the videotape says, "Tragically, Rep. Brooks had been stopped by the chairman [Inouye]. The truth of the matter is that you do have those standby provisions, and the statutory emergency plans are there whereby you could, in the name of stopping terrorism, apprehend, invoke the military, and arrest Americans and hold them in detention camps."

FEMA (Federal Emergency Management Agency) was created as a crisis management agency by Zbigniew Brzezinski and Samuel Huntington. Brzezinski was President Carter's national security advisor, and Huntington was coordinator of security planning for the National Security Council under Brzezinski. Huntington had written the American section of the report, "The Crisis of Democracy," for the Trilateral Commission meeting in Kyoto, Japan, on May 30–31, 1975. And in this document, he advocated crisis management and a stronger role for the president, who shouldn't be "fettered by a chain of picayune restrictions and prohibitions." He endorsed mechanisms of economic planning and further advocated a system in which "areas where democratic procedures are appropriate are limited" because a functioning system requires "some measure of apathy and noninvolvement." This is the typical elitist attitude toward the people.

Ritt Goldstein in his *Sydney Morning-Herald* article mentioned earlier further stated:

When President Ronald Reagan was considering invading Nicaragua he issued a series of executive orders that provided FEMA with broad powers in the event of a "crisis" such as "violent and widespread internal dissent or national opposition against a U.S. military invasion abroad." . . . A *Miami Herald* article on July 5, 1987, reported that the former FEMA director Louis Giuffrida's deputy, John Brinkerhoff, handled the martial law portion of the planning. The plan was said to be similar to one Mr. Giuffrida had developed earlier to combat "a national uprising by black militants." It provided for the detention "of at least 21 million American Negroes" in "assembly centers or relocation camps." Today Mr. Brinkerhoff is with the highly influential Anser Institute for Homeland Security. Following a request by the Pentagon in January 2002 that the U.S. military be allowed the option of deploying troops on American streets, the institute in February published a paper by Mr. Brinkerhoff arguing the legality of this.

In the name of protecting our national security, the FBI has been given wider authority. Critical of this wider authority, Elizabeth Soutter Schwarzer (former press secretary of U.S. Rep. Helen Chenoweth-Hage) wrote in "Security's threat to rights" (*The News & Observer*, June 28, 2002) that

> this week the FBI began to make use of its new powers under the U.S.A. Patriot Act. . . . Unnamed FBI agents have appeared before unnamed judges in secret hearings to obtain secret subpoenas. The subpoenas call for libraries to release information on the reading habits of their patrons. Under the new laws, librarians must comply and they must do so in secret—they are subject to prosecution if they reveal what they have been asked for.

Likewise, in Associated Press writer Pete Yost's article, "FBI's New Authority Draws Criticism" (May 31, 2002), is quoted James X. Dempsey (deputy director of the Center for Democracy and Technology) as claiming: "They are using the terrorism crisis as a cover for a wide range of changes, some of which have nothing to do with terrorism."

Not long after the attacks of September 11, 2001, Professor Francis Boyle (professor of international law at the University of Illinois College of Law, in Champaign) told KPFA (Berkeley, California) radio host Dennis Bernstein on November 14, 2001, that

since September 11th, we have seen one blow against the Constitution after another, after another. Recently, we've had Ashcroft saying that he had, unilaterally, instituted monitoring of attorney–client communications without even informing anyone—he just went
ahead and did it, despite the Fourth Amendment ban on unreason-
able searches and seizures without warrant and the Sixth Amendment right to representation by counsel. . . . What we've seen, since
September 11th, if you add up everything that Ashcroft, Bush, [Al-
berto] Gonzales [White House counsel], and their coterie of Feder-
alist Society lawyers have done here, is a coup d'etat against the
United States Constitution.

Then about two weeks later, on November 30, Michael Ratner (an
international lawyer, who has been a Skelly Wright Fellow at Yale
Law School) wrote "Moving toward a police state (or have we arrived?)," published by the Centre for Research on Globalisation. And
in this essay, he explained that

rights that we thought embedded in the Constitution and protected
by international law are in serious jeopardy or have already been
eliminated. It is no exaggeration to say we are moving toward a
police state. In this atmosphere, we should take nothing for granted. We will not be protected, nor will the courts, the Congress, or
the many liberals who are gleefully jumping on the bandwagon of
repression guarantee our rights.

Along these same lines, Pete Yost, in his article mentioned earlier,
quoted U.S. Rep. John Conyers (the ranking Democrat on the House
Judiciary Committee) as proclaiming: "The administration's contin-
ued defiance of constitutional safeguards seems to have no end in
sight." Later, Kelly Patricia O'Meara wrote "Losing the War for Civil
Liberties" (*Insight,* August 26, 2002), in which she quoted John White-
head (president of the Rutherford Institute) as saying "the only thing

between us and tyranny is the Constitution of the United States. Do I think we've lost civil liberties? Yes. Have we set the groundwork for a police state? Yes." She then quoted Dave Kopel (research director for the Independence Institute) similarly regarding the "USA Patriot Act" stating that "it's not a police state yet, but we're close to it." Also concerning this Act of Congress, she quoted Rep. Ron Paul remarking:

> I think there is a strong determination on the part of government to know everything about everybody, and fighting terrorism is the excuse, not the reason. All of these laws have been in the mill for years, and everything now is in place for what some people describe as a police state. I think we're on the verge of a very, very tough police state in this country.

For a thorough analysis of the potential dangers resulting from the "USA Patriot Act," see *No Greater Threat: America After September 11 and the Rise of a National Security State* (2002) by attorney C. William Michaels.

Less than two weeks after O'Meara's article, the Fort Wayne, Indiana, *Journal-Gazette* editorialized on September 8 in "Attacks on Liberty" that

> in the name of national security, President Bush, Attorney General John Ashcroft, and even Congress have pulled strand after strand out of the constitutional fabric that distinguishes the United States from other nations. . . . Actions taken over the past year are eerily reminiscent of tyranny portrayed in the most nightmarish works of fiction. The power to demand reading lists from libraries could have been drawn from the pages of Ray Bradbury's *Fahrenheit 451*. . . . The sudden suspension of due process for immigrants rounded up into jails is familiar to readers of Sinclair Lewis' *It Can't Happen Here*.

The next month, in the October 21 edition of *The New Republic*, Jeffrey Rosen in "Civil Right: Thank Goodness for Dick Armey" noted:

> "The attorney general doesn't seem to be making an effort to contain the lust for power that these people in the Department of Justice have," Dick Armey, the retiring House Majority Leader, told me. "The Justice Department in the U.S. today, more than any other federal agency, seems to be running amok and out of control. . . . We signaled that Congress is not interested in TIPS [federal program that encourages private employees to spy on their fellow citizens and report suspicious activity to the FBI]," said Armey. "But [the Justice Department's] attitude is, 'We're going to do it anyway.' . . . This agency right now is the biggest threat to personal liberty in the country," he said.

Then in the November-December edition of *Legal Affairs*, its editor and president, Lincoln Caplan, opined in "Secret Affairs" that

> the USA Patriot Act . . . authorized law enforcement agencies to inspect the most personal kinds of information—medical records, bank statements, college transcripts, even church memberships. But what is more startling than the scope of these new powers is that the government can use them on people who aren't suspected of committing a crime.

Dr. Stan Monteith has repeatedly pointed out that while "Homeland Security" measures and the "USA Patriot Act" infringe upon the liberties of American citizens, there has been a glaring lack of certain activities to thwart terrorists. For example, according to National Eagle Forum president Phyllis Schlafly, seventy-nine people whose names were on an FBI watch list were granted visas after the September 11, 2001, attacks. She asked,

Why hasn't anybody been fired for granting [these] visas? Why was the State Department official in charge of issuing visas, Mary Ryan, given a $15,000 "outstanding performance" award for the period that included 9/11? The General Accounting Office reported that 13 of the 19 hijackers were given visas without ever seeing a U.S. consular official, and independent experts said that at least 15 of the 19 hijackers should have been denied visas based on existing law. Why wasn't anybody fired when INS mailed visas to two of the 9/11 hijackers, Mohammed Atta and Marwan Al-Shehhi, on March 5, 2002, six months after they died in their attack on the World Trade Center? President Bush said he was "pretty hot" about that, but he wasn't hot enough to fire anybody. Why does the Bush administration allow the State Department to maintain its ridiculous policy that a history of advocating terrorism is not sufficient to deny an alien a visa?

Additionally, concerning a glaring lack of action to thwart terrorists, the American-Mexican border has not been greatly secured against illegal aliens, despite the fact that Mexico's national security advisor, Adolfo Aguilar, announced that Islamic terrorist organizations have a presence along the U.S. border with the purpose of carrying out guerrilla activities in the U.S. And according to Judith Miller in "Departing Security Official Issues Warning" (*New York Times,* February 2, 2003), President Bush's cybersecurity chief, Richard A. Clarke, after resigning on January 31 informed us that "we still don't have control of our borders, or sufficient control of terrorist money transfers. And we still don't know where all the potential sleeper cells are in the U.S."

Further acknowledging the lack of certain measures to thwart terrorists, the Council on Foreign Relations (CFR) issued a press release on October 25, 2002, which begins with the words: "A year after 9/11, America remains dangerously unprepared to prevent and respond to a catastrophic attack on U.S. soil, concludes a blue-ribbon panel led by former senators Warren Rudman and Gary Hart, co-chairs of the now famous Commission on National Security that warned of such a terrorist attack three years ago." In the panel's report, "America Still Unprepared—America Still in Danger," one learns that

> in all likelihood, the next attack will result in even greater casualties and widespread disruption to American lives and the economy. . . . Only the tiniest percentage of containers, ships, trucks, and trains that enter the United States each day are subject to examination—and a weapon of mass destruction could well be hidden among this cargo. . . . The homeland infrastructure for refining and distributing energy to support the daily lives of Americans remains largely unprotected to sabotage.

Americans would do well to remember some important words from two editorials by a small-town newspaper, *The Press Enterprise*, in Bloomsburg, Pennsylvania. On September 12, 2001 (the day after the terrorist attacks), the editor wrote:

> . . . the real strength of this nation does not reside in its soaring towers, in its great economic engines, or even in its military. At its core, the United States is a set of principles that have become a beacon for the rest of the world. . . . We cannot allow that shining beacon to collapse in a cloud of fear and repression.

Then in a June 1, 2002, editorial, "Is this still the United States?" one reads:

> Sad to say, in the nine months since the attacks, that is what's been happening. Fear for our safety has panicked the public to demand more government protection. . . . When we lose the guarantees and civil rights that define America, we will become like the anti-democratic cultures that spawned the Sept. 11 terrorists. When that happens, they win.

"The guarantees and civil rights that define America" come from our U.S. Constitution. So why then is "make numerous references to U.S. Constitution" on a list of identifiers prepared by the FBI in its Phoenix, Arizona, office, with the suggestion: "If you encounter any of the following, call the Joint Terrorism Task Force"? (See cover page of FBI document with list of identifiers on next page.) And why did this document only cover domestic terrorists, defined as "groups or individuals operating entirely inside the U.S.," thus not including members of al-Qaeda operating inside the U.S. and abroad? And why did an FBI agent in Oklahoma immediately after the attacks of September 11, 2001, call Dr. Stan Monteith of Radio Liberty asking him several questions, including whether Dr. Monteith believed we are in the "end times"? Why is the FBI asking Americans about their religious beliefs?

Perhaps it is important at this point to remember what James MacGregor Burns wrote in *The Power to Lead* (1984). Burns was a university professor who had also been a member of the ACLU and president of the International Society for Political Psychology (and he had done postgraduate work at the London School of Economics, formed by the Fabian Socialists). In this book, Burns proclaimed:

> Let us face reality. The framers [of the U.S. Constitution] have simply been too shrewd for us. They designed separate institutions that cannot be unified by mechanical linkages, frail bridges, tinkering. If we are to "turn the founders upside down," we must directly confront the constitutional structure they erected. . . . I doubt that Americans under normal conditions could agree on the package of radical and "alien" constitutional changes that would be required. They would do so, I think, only during and following a stupendous national crisis and political failure.

Perhaps like a terrorist attack that political leaders did not prevent? Neil Mackay in the ~~Irish~~ *Sunday Herald* (September 15, 2002) wrote

If you encounter

any of the following, Call the Joint Terrorism Task Force

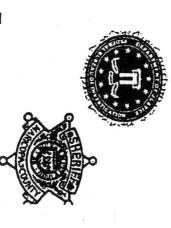

Federal Bureau of Investigation
201 East Indianola Avenue
Phoenix, Arizona 85012

Common Law Movement Proponents

- Fictitious license plates
- No license plates
- Fictitious drivers license
- No drivers license
- Refuse to identify themselves
- Request authority for stop
- Make numerous references to US Constitution
- Claim driving is a right, not a privilege
- Attempt to "police the police"

"Bush planned Iraq 'regime change' before becoming President," which begins with the following words:

A secret blueprint for U.S. global domination . . . uncovered by the *Sunday Herald*, for the creation of a "global Pax Americana" was drawn up for Dick Cheney (now vice-president), Donald Rumsfeld (defense secretary), Paul Wolfowitz (Rumsfeld's deputy), George W. Bush's younger brother Jeb, and Lewis Libby (Cheney's chief of staff). The document, entitled Rebuilding America's Defenses: Strategies, Forces and Resources for a New Century, was written in September 2000 by the neo-conservative think-tank Project for the New American Century (PNAC). The plan . . . says: "The United States has for decades sought to play a more permanent role in Gulf regional security. While the unresolved conflict with Iraq provides the immediate justification, the need for a substantial American force presence in the Gulf transcends the issue of the regime of Saddam Hussein. . . . New methods of attack—electronic, 'nonlethal,' biological—will be more widely available. . . . Combat likely will take place in new dimensions, in space, cyberspace, and perhaps the world of microbes . . . advanced forms of biological warfare that can 'target' specific genotypes may transform biological warfare from the realm of terror to a politically useful tool." . . . Tam Dalyell, the Labour MP . . . said: "This is garbage. . . . This is a blueprint for U.S. world domination—a new world order of their making. These are the thought processes of fantasist Americans who want to control the world. I am appalled that a British Labour Prime Minister [Tony Blair] should have got into bed with a crew which has this moral standing."

Conclusion

What most Americans unfortunately do not realize is that what is happening is the building of "a new world order step by step," in the words of former Soviet leader Mikhail Gorbachev as he addressed more than one thousand business leaders in Harrogate, northern England, on May 31, 2002. This is the goal of the power elite, and the U.S. and U.S.S.R. cooperated in this regard for decades. For example, most people believe that the Korean War was an all-out effort to defeat the Communists. However, General Douglas MacArthur in his *Reminiscences* (1964) related that the Communist Chinese general Lin Piao had written: "I would never have made the attack and risked my men and military reputation if I had not been assured that Washington would restrain General MacArthur from taking adequate retaliatory measures against my lines of supply and communication." And in case one believes this kind of cooperation only occurred decades ago, it is important to note that the U.S. recently cooperated with Russia against U.S. Naval Lt. Cmdr. Jack Daly in his suit for damage to his eyesight from a laser beamed at him from a Russian cargo ship in U.S. waters (listen to Radio Liberty's program for October 18, 2002, and see relevant articles in the *Seattle Post-Intelligencer* for October 18 and 19, 2002).

Nationally syndicated columnist Charley Reese began his June 10, 2002, column with the words: "Most Americans are so steeped in egalitarian thinking that they like to delude themselves that they share in running the country. We ordinary folks, in fact, don't run the country and have a slim-to-none chance of even influencing its direction."

Reese then proceeded to describe "the elite who run the country." And because they "run the country," President Bush in his March 14, 2002, remarks on global development to the Inter-American Development Bank declared that "America supports the international development goals in the U.N. Millennium Declaration" (the controversial Millennium Development Goals are referred to in part IV of my book *September 11 Prior Knowledge*).

Prior to Gorbachev's statement to the business leaders and prior to President Bush's statement pertaining to the U.N. Millennium Declaration, the U.N. hosted a meeting in Johannesburg, South Africa, entitled the World Summit on Sustainable Development, from August 26 to September 4, 2002. At this meeting, Gorbachev's and Maurice Strong's "Earth Charter" (largely drafted by Steven C. Rockefeller, former Vice-President Nelson Rockefeller's son) was presented and placed in "The Ark of Hope" (see photograph below), which was paraded for those in attendance after it had been on display at the U.N. for about two months prior to the meeting. In a 1997 interview with the *Los Angeles Times*, Gorbachev proclaimed: "My hope is

The Ark of Hope, a 49" x 32" x 32" wooden chest was created as a place of refuge for the Earth Charter document. *(Picture and description taken from the* www.ark-of-hope.org/home.html *website)*

that this charter will be a kind of Ten Commandments, a 'Sermon on the Mount,' that provides a guide for human behavior toward the environment in the next century and beyond." And Maurice Strong has similarly stated: "The real goal of the Earth Charter is that it will in fact become like the Ten Commandments." Moreover, if one looks at the design of the Ark of Hope, it seems similar to the design of the Ark of the Covenant into which the real Ten Commandments were placed. This would fit with the new world religion being planned to go along with the world government, replacing the *Holy Bible* with a Mother Gaia spirituality. It would seem to be no coincidence that Mikhail Gorbachev on "The Charley Rose Show" on PBS (October 24, 1996) said: "Cosmos is my god. Nature is my god."

The globalist power elite who "run the world" have included those pursuing the plans of Cecil Rhodes and the Fabian Socialists. Rhodes had formed the secret "Society of the Elect" to "take the government of the whole world," as he put it. Rhodes' followers and the Fabians cooperated at times, and at other times they opposed each other, in their pursuits of power, though both groups had the goal of moving mankind toward a world Socialist government. In fact, this struggle may have been what George Orwell's *1984* was all about. The title, *1984*, came from the centenary of the founding of the Fabian Society. Although Fabian Society co-founders Sidney and Beatrice Webb worked with those elitists pursuing Cecil Rhodes' plans, the Webbs had a certain dislike for those people. According to the 1965 volume of *Current Biography,*

> At the request of Sidney and Beatrice Webb, [Fabian Socialist] Leonard Woolf wrote for the Fabian Society, among other books and pamphlets, *International Government* [1916]. The book, which analyzed precedents and outlined future possibilities for a supernational agency to enforce peace in the world, was one of the major sources consulted by the officials who drew up Britain's proposals for a League of Nations.

Woolf has been called "the father of international government."

Following the League of Nations, the next attempt at international government was the U.N. at the end of World War II. And in Rose Martin's *The Selling of America* (1973), she revealed that

> referring to it [the U.N.], the Honorable Harold Wilson, Parliamentary Leader of the British Labour Party and Fabian Socialism's top spokesman in the councils of the Socialist International, announced with rare frankness in 1964: "We are for World Government, and the United Nations is our instrument!" His declaration was almost identical to that approved by the Oslo Conference of the International two years earlier, which contained the following significant passage: "The ultimate object of the parties of the Socialist International is nothing less than world government. As a first step toward it, they seek to strengthen the United Nations. . . ."

Although *1984* author George Orwell had been a Fabian Socialist, he also worked for press baron Lord Astor (who was pursuing Rhodes' plan) during World War II. Thus, he was probably familiar with both the Rhodes side and the Fabian side of the power struggle. If those pursuing Rhodes' plans are represented by "Big Brother" in *1984*, then perhaps the Fabian Socialists are represented by Emmanuel Goldstein (the traitor against Big Brother) in the book. Neuroscientist David Goodman in "Orwell's 1984: The Future Is Here" (*Insight*, August 19, 2002) said that Sidney Webb "is the physical model for Emmanuel Goldstein," and that although Orwell titled the book *1984*, "a careful review of the literary evidence reveals that he was aiming at the period immediately following the year 2000." This is where we are today, and for an interesting comparison of where we are today and *1984*, read "Learning to love Big Brother: George W. Bush channels George Orwell" (*San Francisco Chronicle*, July 28, 2002) by Daniel Kurtzman.

President George W. Bush and his father and grandfather have all been members of the Yale University secret society Skull and Bones, some of whom have belonged to the globalist power elite who "run the world." On the NBC "Today Show" (September 4, 2002) website, one finds the following excerpt from *Secrets of the Tomb: Skull and Bones, the Ivy League, and the Hidden Paths of Power* by Alexandra Robbins, herself a member of another of Yale's secret societies. In her book, Robbins writes that "much of the way we understand the world of power involves myriad assumptions of connection and control, of cause and effect, and of coincidence that surely cannot be coincidence." She also indicates that after she wrote an article about Skull and Bones in the *Atlantic Monthly* (May 2000), she received a call from a fellow journalist who is a member of Skull and Bones and who scolded her for writing the article. When she wouldn't reveal her sources for information about the society, she wrote that he coldly hissed, "There are a lot of us at newspapers and at political journalism institutions. Good luck with your career," and then he slammed down the phone.

In her book, Robbins looked at the background of Skull and Bones and quoted one Bonesman as saying that the society's founders "were a very adult set of the ruling elite." She then quoted from the 1887 *Yale Illustrated Horoscope*: "No other society has the brazen gall to attempt to crush the will of the majority." Robbins also claimed that "Skull and Bones does not just condone stealing, it actively encourages it (calling it 'crooking something')."

She then described an almost pagan Skull and Bones wedding ceremony where "the Bonesmen wore black, hooded robes, and intoned chants in strange languages. . . . The men waved an object that resembled a baton over a coffin and spoke about ghosts." One Bonesman told her that "the biggest benefit to Skull and Bones is the networking." There have been nine members of the Bush family in Skull and Bones, and when George Herbert Walker Bush became president, he appointed the following Bonesmen: Richard Anthony Moore as ambassador to Ireland, Paul Lambert as ambassador to Ecuador, David George Ball as an assistant secretary of labor, Edward McNally as a speechwriter, former *New York Times* reporter Edwin L. Dale, Jr., as senior advisor to Bush's budget director, as well as other appointees.

Robbins revealed that although George W. Bush has attempted to distance himself from Skull and Bones publicly, "at least 58 Bonesmen contributed at least $57,972 to his presidential bid," and that after he was elected, he had a reunion of Bonesmen from his class of 1968 in the White House. She further noted the following Bonesmen appointed by President George W. Bush: William Howard Taft IV as legal advisor to Secretary of State Colin Powell, Edward McNally as general counsel of the new federal office of Homeland Security, Roy Austin as ambassador to Trinidad and Tobago, Evan G. Galbraith as the defense advisor to the U.S. mission to NATO, and Victor Ashe as board of directors member of the Federal National Mortgage Association (Fannie Mae). More recently, on December 10, 2002, President Bush named Skull and Bones (and CFR) member William Henry Donaldson to be chairman of the Securities and Exchange Commission. Donaldson has been a trustee of the Ford Foundation and the German Marshall Fund, as well as an undersecretary of state and a special consultant and advisor to Vice-President Nelson Rockefeller.

Robbins listed many members of the CIA who are Bonesmen, and indicated that Winston Lord (Bones, 1959) was president of the Council on Foreign Relations from 1977 to 1985. In a September 30, 2002, interview with Dr. Stan Monteith on Radio Liberty, Robbins explained that the purpose of Skull and Bones is "power," and she concluded the interview by stating:

> I want them [readers of her book] to learn that Skull and Bones exists. It is real. It has much more power within America and within the world scene than people believe. And the reason I wrote the book is to get the message out to mainstream America that Skull and Bones is something that we should be fearful of and disturbed by, and only by spreading the truth about this organization will we be able to tear it down.

Bill Clinton's mentor at Georgetown University, Prof. Carroll Quigley, in his book *Tragedy and Hope* (1966), wrote regarding Skull and Bones member William C. Whitney and other members of the power elite toward the end of the nineteenth century:

> They expected that they would be able to control both political parties equally. Indeed, some of them intended to contribute to both and to allow an alternation of the two parties in public office in order to conceal their own influence, inhibit any exhibition of independence by politicians, and to allow the electorate to believe that they were exercising their own free choice.

Recently, there has been an alternation of power with President George H. W. Bush (Skull and Bones member) replaced by President Bill Clinton (Rhodes scholar) replaced by President George W. Bush (Skull and Bones member). However, they all have similar globalist corporate views supporting NAFTA, GATT, and permanent normal trade relations with Communist China.

Initially, Cecil Rhodes' plan was a conspiracy, and early Fabian Socialist H. G. Wells referred to the Fabians' plan as "a plot." However, both of their plans have evolved into what Wells called an "open conspiracy," or a globalist network of like-minded power elite. Relevant to this, Pulitzer Prize-winning journalist Ben Bagdikian in his *The Media Monopoly* (5th edition, 1997) explained:

> Leading corporations own the leading news media and their advertisers subsidize most of the rest. They decide what news and entertainment will be made available to the country; they have direct influence on the country's laws by making the majority of the massive campaign contributions that go to favored politicians; their lobbyists are permanent fixtures in legislatures. This inevitably raises suspicions of overt conspiracy. But there is none. Instead, there is something more insidious: a system of shared values within con-

temporary American corporate culture and corporations' power to extend the culture to the American people, inappropriate as it may be.

The globalist power elite's agenda will be carried forward regardless of the alternation of power by the two major political parties. According to Prof. Quigley, this would be ideal, as he wrote in *Tragedy and Hope:*

> The argument that the two parties should represent opposed ideals and policies, one, perhaps, of the Right and the other of the Left, is a foolish idea acceptable only to doctrinaire and academic thinkers. Instead, the two parties should be almost identical, so that the American people can "throw the rascals out" at any election without leading to any profound or extensive shifts in policy.

Bill Clinton's way of blending "the Right" and "the Left" was called "the Third Way." And relevant to George W. Bush, Dana Milbank in the February 1, 2001, *Washington Post* wrote, "Needed: Catchword for Bush Ideology; 'Communitarianism' Finds Favor," in which one reads:

> . . . Some Bush advisors and friends say . . . his actions have less to do with the left vs. the right than with his embrace of many of the ideas contained in the movement known as "communitarianism," which places the importance of society ahead of the unfettered rights of the individual. "This is the ultimate Third Way," said Don Eberly, an advisor in the Bush White House, using a favorite phrase of President Bill Clinton. . . . Bush's inaugural address, said George Washington University professor Amitai Etzioni, a communitarian thinker, "was a communitarian text." . . . That's no accident: Bush's advisors consulted on the speech with Robert D. Putnam of Harvard University (a leading communitarian thinker). At the same time,

> Bush has recruited some of the leading thinkers of the "civil soci-
> ety," or "communitarian," movements to his White House. . . . Top
> Bush strategist Karl Rove introduced Bush to the thinking.

Many people scoff at the idea that there is a "power elite" who are leading us. However, in *Global Challenges for Humanity*, published by the American Council for the United Nations University in the year A.D. 2000, one reads under "North America" that "the region is led by power elites." The globalist power elite's goal is "one world," and in case one doesn't believe the American public is being conditioned to accept this concept, reflect upon the fact that Poudre High School in Fort Collins, Colorado, has never played the national anthem at its graduation ceremony. However, in A.D. 2002 the school played "The World Anthem" with the idea of "one people, one world" and closing lyrics of "All as one for all." And according to an interview by staff writer Todd Hartman in the *Rocky Mountain News* (June 7, 2002), "the Air Force's Band of the Rockies is taken with the piece and arranging its own version. It's slated to be played at . . . a ceremony celebrating the 40th anniversary of the Peace Corps this summer."

It is in our public schools that a great deal of damage has been done to the values upon which this nation was founded, and Christian leaders bear a significant responsibility for this. When Bible reading and prayer were removed from the public schools in the early 1960s, the Supreme Court said that was required because of "separation of church and state" and that government should remain "neutral" in areas of religious beliefs or lack thereof. What Christian leaders then failed (and still fail today) to point out is that when public schools teach values and God is not the authority for teaching what is right and wrong, then this is *not* government neutrality but rather *discrimination* by the government against the biblical morality most parents are teaching at home, because an authority (e.g., majority opinion, autonomous moral decision-makers, etc.) other than God is controlling.

Relevant to the attacks of September 11, 2001, if there will ultimately be a "Big Brother" who will take away our freedom and human rights, you might ask yourself, "Why would Osama bin Laden
be helping to usher in his reign?" In CNN's "Bin Laden's sole post-
September 11 TV interview aired" (February 5, 2002), referring to
bin Laden's interview by the Arabic-language Al-Jazeera network on
October 21, 2002, Osama bin Laden is quoted as saying: "I tell you,
freedom and human rights in America are doomed. The U.S. government will lead the American people in—and the West in general—
into an unbearable hell and a choking life."

What we have been subjected to in general for decades is the
process of mass psychology. And in that regard, Fabian Socialist Ber-
trand Russell in *The Impact of Science on Society* (1953) declared:

> I think the subject which will be of most importance politically is
> mass psychology. . . . Although this science will be diligently stud-
> ied, it will be rigidly confined to the governing class. The populace
> will not be allowed to know how its convictions were generated.
> When the technique has been perfected, every government that has
> been in charge of education for a generation will be able to control
> its subjects securely without the need of armies or policemen. . . .
> Educational propaganda, with government help, could achieve this
> result in a generation. . . . There are, however, two powerful forces
> opposed to such a policy: one is religion; the other is nationalism.
> . . . Population can be kept from increasing. . . . Perhaps bacterio-
> logical war may prove effective. . . . A scientific world society can-
> not be stable unless there is a world government.

St. George Tucker (member of the Virginia State Supreme Court, 1803–
1811) cautioned: "The ignorance of the people is the footstool of despotism." Pray that Americans will shed their ignorance and defend
the God-given rights upon which this nation—this constitutional republic—was founded, resisting the new world order despotism of the

globalist power elite. And pray for the families of the victims of September 11 (for information on how they may be helped, see two websites: [1] *www.familiesofseptember11.org* and [2] *www.voicesofsept11.org*).

Ending on a somewhat personal note, throughout my father's life he often repeated the quote, "Hope springs eternal." Though he suffered much during his life on this earth—ruptured appendix and (during World War II) malaria and other sufferings, later melanoma cancer and skin grafts, and four heart attacks, he always retained "hope" and never complained. His daily life was "spent" for others. In his wallet he always carried the reminder, "The last enemy that shall be destroyed is death" (1 Corinthians 15:26) and the prayer, "But thou hast saved us from our enemies, and hast put them to shame that hated us. In God we boast all the day long, and praise thy name for ever. . . . Out of the depths have I cried unto thee, O Lord. Lord, hear my voice: let thine ears be attentive to the voice of my supplications" (Ps. 44:7–8; 130:1–2).

As this book is being published, the diplomatic phase of "the process" is still ongoing, and it is uncertain whether there will be a war with Iraq. Though there have been protests in cities around the world against such a war, President Bush has, to date, sent about three hundred thousand American troops to the Middle East in preparation for war against Iraq, or—as some news media term it—a "Showdown with Saddam" Hussein.

But whatever happens in the future, we should pray daily and with sincere hearts to God, our only real and Eternal Hope. And we should also take some concrete action, such as encouraging our local public schools across the nation to display our national motto. See the example on the following page of what the people in one school district did, and duplicate their effort nationwide.

CUMBERLAND COUNTY POSTS NATIONAL MOTTO POSTERS

By Reverend Mark H. Creech

For almost a year the Cumberland County School Board demurred about applying state law and posting the national motto in its public schools. So the Cumberland County American Family Association (CCAFA) applied pressure the old-fashioned way – by appealing to the public. CCAFA President Jeff Long said the School Board kept dodging a resolution to encourage the district's teachers to post a copy of the national motto "In God We Trust," although state law gave the board authority to do so. The posters had been donated to the school district. "When the Board balked, local radio stations picked up the story and chided the School Board publicly," said Long. "You can imagine how upset people got, especially those who serve in the military."

CCAFA's appeal to the public resulted in action by County School Superintendent William C. Harrison. Harrison announced at the School Board meeting of October 8 that he was sending a notice to all principals that they were at liberty to order free national motto posters from CCAFA to display in their schools. The next day, the media descended on Cumberland County, public schools capturing film footage of teachers standing proudly before bare spots on classroom walls proclaiming: "This is where we will hang ours when it arrives." One of the county's high schools ordered 150 posters; a middle school asked for 80 - and more orders are still coming in over a month later.

One local radio station, WFNC, congratulated CCAFA for what it conceded must be "a satisfying outcome for them in their yearlong pursuit to get permission to have the motto posted." Station manager Jeff Thompson added that he was pleased to be able to view their own national motto poster provided by CCAFA and hanging on WFNC's newsroom wall. The station also conducted a call-in poll to sample listeners' reactions to the motto's display. The result was an astonishing 95.6 percent in favor of the Superintendent's action; the highest favorable result registered on any polling issue the news talk station had conducted.

In correspondence sent to the Christian Action League, Long wrote: "We must resolve in this critical hour to teach the bedrock fundamentals of our nation's unique civic, social, and legal history as well as our Judeo-Christian heritage or America will shortly be consigned to the dustbin of history. North Carolina lawmakers wisely foresaw this likelihood and gave us education laws allowing our national motto and other important documents to be prominently displayed in our public schools. The objective is to see that our children are familiar with them and are inspired evermore to contemplate their deeper significance to our nation. If we fail to ensure that these laws are put into effect, we will have betrayed our posterity. Therefore, let us move with haste to see that our national motto is displayed in as many classrooms as possible across our great State."

Addendum

Concerning all of the subjects mentioned in this book, one of the most important elements in considering any of them is to what extent can the government be believed. In that regard, Scott Peterson, staff writer of the *Christian Science Monitor*, in the article "In war, some facts less factual" (September 6, 2002), revealed that

shortly before U.S. strikes began in the [1991] Gulf War, the *St. Petersburg Times* asked two experts to examine the satellite images of the Kuwait and Saudi Arabia border area taken in mid-September 1990, a month and a half after the Iraqi invasion. "That [Iraqi build-up] was the whole justification for Bush sending troops in there, and it just didn't exist," Ms. [Jean] Heller [*St. Petersburg Times*] says. Three times Heller contacted the office of Secretary of Defense Dick Cheney [now vice-president] for evidence refuting the *Times* photos or analysis—offering to hold the story if proven wrong. The official response: "Trust us." To this day, the Pentagon's photographs of the Iraqi troop buildup remain classified. . . . John MacArthur, publisher of *Harper's Magazine* and author of *Second Front: Censorship and Propaganda in the Gulf War*, says that considering the number of senior officials shared by both Bush administrations, the American public should bear in mind the lessons of Gulf War propaganda. "These are all the same people who were running it more than 10 years ago," Mr. MacArthur says. "They'll make up just about anything . . . to get their way." . . . In the fall of 1990, members of

Congress and the American public were swayed by the tearful testimony of a 15-year-old Kuwaiti girl, known only as Nayirah. In the girl's testimony before a congressional caucus, well-documented in MacArthur's book *Second Front* and elsewhere, she described how, as a volunteer in a Kuwait maternity ward, she had seen Iraqi troops storm her hospital, steal the incubators, and leave 312 babies "on the cold floor to die." Seven U.S. senators later referred to the story during debates; the motion for war passed by just five votes. In the weeks after Nayirah spoke, President Bush senior invoked the incident five times, saying that such "ghastly atrocities" were like "Hitler revisited." . . . Later, it was learned that Nayirah was in fact the daughter of the Kuwaiti ambassador to Washington and had no connection to the Kuwaiti hospital. She had been coached—along with a handful of others who would "corroborate" the story—by senior executives of Hill and Knowlton in Washington, the biggest global PR firm at the time, which had a contract worth more than $10 million with the Kuwaitis to make the case for war.

Another important element is who is behind the current push toward war with Iraq. In Ben Wattenberg's "More feck, less hoc" (*Jewish World Review,* April 16, 2001), he asked: "So what might be the basis of an American foreign policy?" He then described a 1992 Department of Defense "Defense Planing Guidance" classified document written by then department undersecretary for policy Paul Wolfowitz and his deputy I. Lewis "Scooter" Libby advocating a policy "that at its core was to guard against the emergence of hostile regional superpowers, for example, Iraq or China. Such regional vigilance, they believed, would prevent the rise of a hostile global superpower."

Paul Wolfowitz is now deputy defense secretary, and on February 1, 2003, the *New York Times* published "The Brains Behind Bush's War Policy" by Todd Purdum describing "a group that history may remember for the concept of the preemptive attack." The article begins with these words:

Any history of the Bush administration's march toward war with Iraq will have to take account of long years of determined advocacy by a circle of defense policy intellectuals whose view that Saddam Hussein can no longer be tolerated or contained is now ascendant. . . . At the center of this group are longtime Iraq hawks, Republicans like Deputy Defense Secretary Paul D. Wolfowitz; Richard Perle, a former Reagan administration defense official who now heads the Defense Policy Board, the Pentagon's advisory panel; and William Kristol, who was chief of staff to Vice-President Dan Quayle and now edits the conservative *Weekly Standard.*

The article later refers to "Robert Kagan, a scholar at the Carnegie Endowment for International Peace, [as] the co-author of a December 1, 1997, editorial with Mr. Kristol in *The Weekly Standard,* to which Mr. Wolfowitz contributed an article. The cover headline: 'Saddam Must Go.'" And toward the end of Purdum's article, he indicates that Mr. Kristol and Lawrence Kaplan are the authors of a forthcoming book, *The War Over Iraq: Saddam's Tyranny and America's Mission.* And he refers to Mr. Kristol's Project for the New American Century, begun in 1997, with the group the next year (1998) "urging Mr. Clinton to adopt a 'full complement' of diplomatic and military measures to remove Mr. Hussein, in a letter signed by Mr. Wolfowitz, Defense Secretary Donald H. Rumsfeld, and others who now hold senior administration jobs."

The Project is an initiative of the New Citizenship Project, with William Kristol as chairman, and CFR members Robert Kagan, Devon Gaffney Cross, Bruce F. Jackson, and John R. Bolton as directors, and Paul Wolfowitz among the Project participants. Robert Kagan is the author of the new book *Of Paradise and Power: America and Europe in the New World Order.* In September 2000, the Project issued a report, "Rebuilding America's Defenses," co-chaired by Donald Kagan (CFR member) and Gary Schmitt. And in the report one reads that the United States has for decades sought to play a more permanent role in Gulf regional security. While the unresolved conflict with Iraq provides the immediate justification, the need for a substantial American force presence in the Gulf transcends the issue of the regime of Saddam Hussein. . . . Further, the process of transformation, even if it brings revolutionary change, is likely to be a long one, absent some catastrophic and catalyzing event—like a new Pearl Harbor. . . . We cannot allow North Korea, Iran, Iraq, or similar states to undermine American leadership, intimidate American allies, or threaten the American homeland itself.

Would not a war with Iraq afford the U.S. "a more permanent role in Gulf regional security" even after the "regime of Saddam Hussein" is gone? And wasn't the terrorist attack of September 11, 2001, "a catastrophic and catalyzing event" compared by many to "Pearl Harbor"? And did not President George W. Bush begin calling North Korea, Iran, and Iraq "the axis of evil" and saying that we need "homeland security"?

On September 15, 1999, the United States Commission on National Security/21st Century issued a report, "New World Coming: American Security in the 21st Century." The commission is chaired by former U.S. senators Gary Hart and Warren Rudman, and includes CFR president Leslie Gelb among its commissioners. In this report, one reads that

disaffected groups will acquire weapons of mass destruction and mass disruption, and some will use them. Americans will likely die on American soil, possibly in large numbers. . . . Global forces, especially economic ones, will continue to batter the concept of national sovereignty. The state, as we know it, will also face challenges to its sovereignty under the mandate of evolving international law and by disaffected groups, including terrorists and criminals.

Then on April 15, 2000, the same commission issued another report,

"Seeking a National Strategy: A Concert for Preserving Security and Promoting Freedom," in which one reads about terrorists and those possessing weapons of mass destruction that

> the magnitude of the danger posed by weapons of mass destruction compels this nation to consider carefully the means and circumstances of preemption. . . . The United States must be willing to lead in assembling ad hoc coalitions outside of U.N. auspices of necessary. . . . The United States has a continuing critical interest in keeping the Persian Gulf secure, and . . . it must be a high priority to prevent either Iraq or Iran from deploying deliverable weapons of mass destruction.

Didn't a large number of Americans die on American soil due to terrorist attacks? Hasn't the economic impact of the World Trade Organization battered the concept of national sovereignty? And hasn't President George W. Bush talked about taking preemptive action against Iraq because of its weapons of mass destruction?